Praise for *Say It With Me*

"Comprehensive, practical, and immediately usable, *Say It With Me* seamlessly bridges the worlds of Speech Pathology and Applied Behavior Analysis. Rose offers insights that will benefit both new and experienced clinicians and educators alike."

> —**Sasha Long, M.A., BCBA**, founder and president, The Autism Helper, Inc.

"Speech-language pathologists supporting emergent communicators know how challenging it can be to identify the most effective path forward for students who are not yet speaking and may also present with complex behaviors. In *Say It With Me*, Rose Griffin offers clinicians a practical and refreshing guide grounded in naturalistic strategies, real-world examples, and the power of multidisciplinary collaboration. Her dual expertise as both an SLP and BCBA provides a uniquely integrated perspective that helps professionals better understand the intersection of communication and behavior. This book is an invaluable resource for clinicians seeking thoughtful, actionable tools to spark meaningful communication and social engagement for our clients who need it most."

> —**Calonda Henry, M.S., CCC-SLP**, founder and CEO,
> Broad Horizons Speech Therapy

"This book is an exceptional contribution to the field, offering a well-integrated approach that aligns clinical rigor with compassionate, relationship-centered care. It provides practical frameworks that support communication, regulation, and meaningful skill development across settings. I would highly recommend *Say It With Me* to multidisciplinary teams, educators, and families seeking effective, respectful strategies."

> —**Dr. Jocelyn M. Geib, PhD, CCC/SLP**, speech and language pathologist,
> educational consultant, and executive director of The KidsLink School;
> director of therapy at the KidsLink Neurobehavioral Center

"Rose shares a compassionate path forward in helping all students find a way to communicate. This is a great read for parents and professionals alike."

> —**Jacqueline Laurita**

"Finally, a book with a step-by-step guide to conduct more effective speech therapy sessions for autistic clients like my son. As a mom to a child with nonverbal autism and apraxia, I have often felt like I have the only child that struggles immensely with speech therapy. And I know that his therapists have often felt unproductive and even confused as well. Instead of avoiding, *Say It With Me* dives right into effective interventions that will help with the common frustrations that speech therapists can face. This is a must read for all the SLPs, BCBAs, and RBTs working with children like mine. Thank you, Rose!"

> —**Kate Swenson**, author of national bestseller *Forever Boy* and
> *New York Times* bestseller *Autism Out Loud*

Say It With Me

Say It With Me

NATURALISTIC TOOLS
TO SPARK SPEECH AND SOCIAL ENGAGEMENT
FOR EMERGENT COMMUNICATORS

ROSE GRIFFIN
MA, CCC-SLP, BCBA

JB JOSSEY-BASS™

A Wiley Brand

*To the students I've had the honor of serving and the passionate
colleagues who walk this path with me.*

Contents

Acknowledgments

I am deeply grateful to the many students and families I have had the privilege of working with in schools and clinics in Cleveland, Ohio, and Austin, Texas. Your trust and collaboration have shaped my understanding of what meaningful, functional communication can look like in real life.

I also extend my sincere thanks to the colleagues who became lifelong friends through countless conversations in shared offices—conversations centered on how to better support all students in finding their voice. Every professional experience, both positive and challenging, has contributed to who I am today.

Thank you to my parents, Benedetto and Mary Ann Donatelli, for their unwavering encouragement through every adventure. Finally, I am grateful to G, Lettie, Pax, and Patrick for their continued support and for all that comes with building and running ABA Speech.

Introduction

I wanted to write the book I wish I'd had when I first started in the field. I was a new speech therapist working with students who were not yet speaking, and I felt like I couldn't reach them—like I wasn't doing enough.

Take a deep breath and know that I am here to cheer you on in this important work you are doing. This book will give you a simple-to-use framework so you can help all of your students find a way to communicate with the world.

You're reading this book because you want to help your students find their voice. But how can you reach every student? What about the students who aren't responding to traditional therapy? The ones who have a hard time engaging in therapy activities?

What if I told you that by reading this book and applying these strategies to your therapy, you could eliminate the overwhelm you're feeling? That you could walk into every therapy session with confidence? That you would see a path forward for all the students on your caseload?

I'm telling you this because you can. You're ready to use these strategies to support all the students on your current caseload—and students you haven't even met yet.

This book is based on science and real-world applications of that science in therapy rooms over the past 20+ years. As both a speech-language pathologist and a board-certified behavior analyst, I've had the unique opportunity to bridge two worlds that don't always speak the same language—but should. I've created a practical, detail-oriented guide to help you feel supported in the important work you do each and every day.

If you're like most speech therapists, you may not have learned about:

1. How to support students who engage in behavioral barriers to therapy
2. Ways to reach students who don't engage in therapy activities
3. How to get started with AAC

This book will be your guide. At times we can feel alone in this work. You might be the only SLP on your campus or in your clinic, but you are not alone. I will be here cheering you on.

Now, let's begin this journey to communication for all students.

CHAPTER 1

From Scores to Solutions: The Assessment Approach That Changes Your Therapy Plan

I remember my first year as a speech therapist, trying to assess a student who was hesitant to come back to the therapy room. I really struggled with how to reach this student. I knew that he was not going to sit or participate in structured and standardized assessment tasks, but I still needed to try and get a baseline of his current communication skills. I felt very, very discouraged. I needed someone to show me that assessment can include a variety of tools. I tried to have him roll a ball back and forth—that didn't work. I attempted having him sit and point to pictures on my test protocol—that didn't work. I gave him free time to play in my therapy room but he wanted to play alone; anytime I came close to his toys, he moved on to something different. I felt utterly defeated.

From this student and many others, I learned that using a combination of standardized and more informal assessments can give us a good snapshot of our student's communication skills at baseline. This true baseline will give us a better understanding of how to plan intervention so that all students can start communicating today.

This chapter and this book will help you feel more confident in knowing that you are reaching each student that you work with. I don't want you to feel overwhelmed like I did; I want you to feel empowered!

I am going to outline not only the speech therapist's role but also the role of other potential people in the assessment process. Whether you are school-based or working in a clinical setting, our evaluations are usually done with team effort. I will share information about collaborative assessment, specific assessments that have helped me as a treating clinician, case studies for various age groups, and the chapter will end with the informal assessments I have created and use in my therapy room. These assessments were developed and are utilized by the members of the ABA Speech Connection. Our connection members use these tools to supplement their current assessment protocols. Let's get started.

Assessment serves as the foundation for effective intervention planning for autistic learners. According to Koenig and Murphy, "the purpose of assessment for learners with ASD (Autism Spectrum Disorders) is to address concerns about increasing communication repertoires and decreasing challenging behaviors that interfere with learning."[1] This fundamental principle underscores the importance of adopting a comprehensive, collaborative assessment approach that considers the whole child and their unique needs.

This chapter explores evidence-based assessment practices for autistic learners across the lifespan, from early childhood through adolescence. We will discuss various assessment tools, collaborative team approaches, and strategies for ensuring that assessment results translate into meaningful intervention planning.

This chapter aims to provide the step-by-step guidance that many clinicians and parents seek when beginning the assessment process with autistic learners, particularly those who are just beginning to develop communication skills.

COLLABORATIVE ASSESSMENT

Collaborative assessment brings together professionals from different disciplines to comprehensively evaluate an autistic learner's strengths and needs. This approach recognizes that autism affects multiple domains of functioning and that no single professional possesses all the expertise needed to conduct a complete assessment.

Steps for Effective Collaboration

For effective collaboration during the assessment process, teams should:

1. **Determine appropriate assessment procedures at intake.**
   - Establish which team members will administer which assessments.
   - Clearly define each professional's role in the process.
   - Avoid last-minute additions to assessment plans.
2. **Establish a timeline for assessment.**
   - Create a schedule that allows sufficient time for thorough evaluation.
   - Consider the learner's attention span and ability to stay on task.
   - Plan for multiple sessions if you can.

3. **Discuss assessment results and intervention goals together.**
   - Schedule team meetings to review findings collectively.
   - Consider virtual meetings to accommodate busy schedules.
   - Ensure all team members have access to assessment reports.
4. **Customize the intervention plan based on assessment findings.**
   - Use assessment data to identify priority targets.
   - Consider the individual's profile rather than using a one-size-fits-all approach.
   - Incorporate family priorities and concerns.

The Role Players

Speech-Language Pathologist

Speech-language pathologists (SLPs) play a crucial role in the assessment of autistic learners. Their evaluation typically focuses on:

- Receptive and expressive language skills
- Pragmatic language and social communication
- Speech production and intelligibility
- Augmentative and alternative communication needs

SLPs bring specialized knowledge about communication development and disorders to the assessment team. Many SLPs work in multiple settings, including public schools, private clinics, and early intervention programs, allowing them to develop expertise across various contexts.

Behavior Analyst

Board certified behavior analysts (BCBAs) contribute important assessment information regarding:

- Functional behavior assessment (FBA) to identify the purpose of challenging behaviors
- Verbal behavior assessment to analyze communication skills from a behavioral perspective
- Analysis of behavioral barriers to learning
- Evaluation of prompt dependency and instructional control

While SLPs and BCBAs have distinct roles, their collaboration is essential for developing a comprehensive understanding of the autistic learner's communication profile and designing effective interventions.

Occupational Therapist

Occupational therapists (OTs) provide a unique perspective in autism assessment by evaluating how sensory processing, motor skills, and daily functioning impact a child's participation in everyday activities.

Key Assessment Areas

1. Sensory processing assessment:
   - Evaluates how the child processes and responds to sensory information
   - Identifies sensory sensitivities or seeking behaviors
   - Assesses sensory regulation abilities and their impact on attention, behavior, and learning
   - Often uses standardized tools like the Sensory Profile or Sensory Processing Measure
2. Motor skills evaluation:
   - Assesses fine motor skills (handwriting, using utensils, manipulating small objects)
   - Evaluates gross motor skills (coordination, balance, strength)
   - Examines motor planning and praxis (ability to conceptualize, plan, and execute new movements)
   - May use tools like the Bruininks-Oseretsky Test of Motor Proficiency or the Developmental Test of Visual-Motor Integration
3. Functional skills assessment:
   - Evaluates self-care skills (dressing, grooming, feeding)
   - Assesses play skills and peer interactions
   - Examines classroom functioning and participation
   - Observes adaptive responses to environmental demands
4. Environmental analysis:
   - Evaluates how the physical environment affects the child's functioning
   - Identifies environmental barriers or supports
   - Assesses the need for adaptations or accommodations

School Psychologist

School psychologists bring expertise in cognitive, academic, behavioral, and social-emotional functioning to the autism assessment process.

Key Assessment Areas

1. Cognitive and developmental assessment:
    *   Evaluates intellectual functioning and cognitive profile
    *   Assesses verbal and nonverbal reasoning abilities
    *   Examines information processing, attention, and executive functioning
    *   May use tools like the WISC, DAS, or KABC
2. Academic functioning:
    *   Assesses impact of autism characteristics on academic performance
    *   Evaluates learning style and educational needs
    *   Identifies academic strengths and challenges
    *   May use achievement tests or curriculum-based assessments
3. Social-emotional and behavioral assessment:
    *   Evaluates social skills and peer relationships
    *   Assesses emotional regulation and understanding
    *   Examines behavioral functioning and adaptive behavior
    *   Often uses tools like the ADOS-2, CARS-2, GARS, or ADI-R
4. Mental health screening:
    *   Screens for co-occurring conditions (anxiety, depression, ADHD)
    *   Assesses impact of autism on mental health and well-being

Assessment Methods

*   Standardized psychological and educational testing
*   Behavioral observations across settings
*   Interviews with parents, teachers, and the student
*   Rating scales and questionnaires
*   Record review (academic history, previous evaluations, medical records)

Parent and Family Involvement

Parents and family members are essential partners in the assessment process. They provide crucial information about:

*   The child's developmental history
*   Communication patterns across different environments
*   Preferences and interests that can be leveraged during the assessment
*   Concerns and priorities for intervention

Teachers

Teachers provide invaluable information during the autism assessment process due to their daily interactions with the child in academic and social contexts. Their observations and insights offer a comprehensive view of how autism characteristics manifest in the educational environment.

CLASSROOM PERFORMANCE DOCUMENTATION

Aspects to Document

Academic Performance

- **Subject-specific functioning:** Detailed information about performance across different academic domains (reading, math, writing, science)
- **Learning style preferences:** Observations about how the student best processes and retains information
- **Task persistence and attention:** Data on the student's ability to focus and complete tasks
- **Response to instructional approaches:** Insights into which teaching methods are most effective
- **Work samples:** Examples of classwork that demonstrate academic strengths and challenges
- **Curriculum-based assessments:** Informal measures of academic skills

Behavioral Observations

- **Classroom behavior patterns:** Documentation of typical behaviors, triggers, and responses
- **Structured vs. unstructured time:** Comparison of functioning during different types of activities
- **Transition abilities:** Observations about how the student handles changes in routines or activities
- **Repetitive behaviors or interests:** Documentation of frequency, duration, and impact on learning
- **Response to sensory aspects of the classroom:** Notes on reactions to noise, lighting, touch, etc.
- **Behavioral incidents:** Records of challenging behaviors and their contexts
- **Behavior management strategies:** Information about effective and ineffective approaches

Social Functioning

- **Peer relationships:** Observations of interactions with classmates
- **Social initiation and response:** Data on how the student engages with others
- **Group work participation:** Information about functioning in collaborative learning situations
- **Playground/recess interactions:** Observations in less-structured social settings
- **Understanding of social rules:** Insights into grasp of implicit social expectations
- **Communication patterns:** Notes on how the student communicates with peers and adults
- **Perspective-taking abilities:** Observations of empathy and understanding others' viewpoints

Adaptive Functioning

- **Classroom independence:** Information about self-management and autonomy
- **Organizational skills:** Observations about materials management and task planning
- **Following routines:** Data on adherence to classroom procedures
- **Self-advocacy skills:** Documentation of ability to seek help or clarification
- **Problem-solving approaches:** Insights into how the student addresses challenges
- **Adaptive technology use:** Information about assistive technology needs or benefits

Assessment Methods Teachers Use

1. **Direct observation:** Systematic recording of behaviors in various classroom contexts
2. **Rating scales:** Completion of standardized questionnaires specific to autism or behavioral characteristics
3. **Anecdotal records:** Ongoing documentation of significant behaviors or events
4. **Functional behavior assessment:** Analysis of behavior patterns to identify triggers and functions
5. **Curriculum-based assessment:** Informal evaluation of academic skills within the current curriculum
6. **Student work analysis:** Systematic review of work samples to identify patterns or challenges

Documentation Teachers May Provide

- **Educational history:** Summary of previous educational experiences and interventions
- **Response to intervention data:** Information about previously implemented supports and their effectiveness

- **Individualized education plan (IEP) progress:** Documentation of progress toward existing goals
- **Behavior intervention plan data:** Records from any existing behavior management approaches
- **Communication log:** History of parent communications about concerns
- **Developmental milestones:** Observations of developmental progress in the educational setting
- **Comparative perspective:** Insights into how the student functions relative to same-age peers

The assessment information from all team members can be integrated to provide the following information:

1. Determine if the child meets diagnostic criteria for autism or another disability category.
2. Identify the child's unique profile of strengths and needs.
3. Develop appropriate intervention goals and strategies.
4. Design individualized education plans and accommodations.
5. Make recommendations for home and community supports.

This collaborative approach ensures a comprehensive understanding of the child and leads to more effective intervention planning.

STANDARDIZED AND CRITERION-REFERENCED TESTS

Now that we have discussed who may do what, let's do a deeper dive into the role that speech-language pathologists play on the assessment team. Like I mentioned, a robust assessment protocol for autistic learners should and may include multiple components. This section discusses some of the most widely used assessments and shares some others (from the BCBA part of my brain) that may be new to you.

Following are some examples of standardized and criterion-referenced tests. I will go into more detail about what these tests measure and how they can be used for a comprehensive assessment.

Standardized assessments compare an individual's performance to same-age peers and may include:

- *Clinical Evaluation of Language Fundamentals* (CELF-5)[2]
- *Expressive One-Word Picture Vocabulary Test*, 4th edition (EOWPVT)[3]
- *Receptive One-Word Picture Vocabulary Test*, 4th edition (ROWPVT)[4]
- *Arizona Test of Articulation*, 4th edition [5]

Criterion-referenced assessments measure performance against predetermined skill criteria and may include:

- Rossetti Infant-Toddler Language Scale[6]
- Early Start Denver Model (ESDM) Curriculum Checklist[7]
- Verbal Behavior Milestones Assessment and Placement Program (VB-MAPP)[8]
- Assessment of Functional Living Skills (AFLS)[9]
- Essential for Living (EFL)[10]

We discuss the primary assessments in this chapter.

Standardized Assessment Tools

When I am working with students who are school-age (5–12 years), I find the following assessment tools to be very helpful.

Clinical Evaluation of Language Fundamentals (CELF-5)

- Developed by Elisabeth H. Wiig, PhD, Eleanor Semel, EdD, Wayne A. Secord, PhD
- Appropriate for children ages 5–21
- Evaluates various aspects of language including:
  - core language (overall language ability)
  - receptive language (understanding and comprehension)
  - expressive language (production and use)
  - language structure (grammar and sentence formation)
  - language content (vocabulary and word knowledge)
  - pragmatic language (social language skills)

As a school-based clinician, I use this assessment often for students who are using some spontaneous language throughout their day.

Expressive One-Word Picture Vocabulary Test, 4th edition

- Developed by Rick Brownell and Nancy A. Martin
- Assesses naming ability for objects, actions, and concepts
- Provides information about expressive vocabulary development

Receptive One-Word Picture Vocabulary Test, 4th edition

- Developed by Rick Brownell and Nancy A. Martin
- Evaluates comprehension of single words
- Requires pointing to pictures in response to verbal stimuli

I like to use both the EOWPVT and the ROWPVT for students of varying language abilities. These tests can give us great insight with less verbal output needed.

Arizona Test of Articulation—4th edition

- Developed by Janet B. Fudala, PhD, and Sheri Stegall, PhD
- Assesses speech sound production
- Identifies articulation and phonological patterns

This can be a nice baseline for students who are able to say a word after you. Not all emerging communicators may be ready to work on articulation but when doing a comprehensive evaluation, I sometimes include this.

Other Helpful Assessments

Communication Matrix

- Developed by Dr. Charity Rowland
- Online assessment tool for individuals at early stages of communication
- Based on four reasons to communicate: refusing, obtaining, social interaction, and information exchange
- Particularly useful for individuals with complex communication needs

I remember the first time I discovered the Communication Matrix.[11] I was set to do a three-year reevaluation for a student in elementary school. The student had a rare genetic disorder and could not use their hands. The student was also nonverbal and had daily seizures. I wanted to capture a true baseline of communicating for this student, but I knew that none of tools that I have previously mentioned would be the right fit. I stumbled across the Communication Matrix, and it has been a reliable tool ever since. I filled this out with the student's teacher, parent, and paraprofessional. It gave us robust information about the student's current communication and helped us develop a functional path forward.

Functional Communication Profile—Revised

- Developed by Larry I. Kleiman
- Comprehensive assessment of communication skills
- Evaluates sensory, motor, attentiveness, receptive language, social language, speech, voice, and fluency

The Functional Communication Profile has been a lifesaver for me.[12] I used it the first time when I was tasked with evaluating a student who had a dual diagnosis of Down syndrome and autism. I was working in a clinic, and I had two hours to administer an assessment—eek! Despite feeling a little scrunched on time, this assessment allowed me to develop a functional communication plan for my student. The parents were happy to read all the skills that the student could do and see an outline of what our intervention would entail. For students who may not have the task duration for a standardized assessment, the Functional Communication Profile—Revised can be an asset!

Criterion-referenced Assessment Tools

When I am working with students who are birth to five years, I find the following assessment tools to be very helpful.

Rossetti Infant-Toddler Language Scale

- Age range: 0–36 months
- Developed by Louis Rossetti, PhD
- Evaluates preverbal and verbal aspects of communication
- Includes parent interview component
- Assesses interaction, attachment, pragmatics, gestures, play, language comprehension, and language expression

This is such a wonderful assessment to give for our youngest learners. At ABA Speech we provide teletherapy to autistic learners in Washington state. The students we support are very young. When I was providing direct therapy, I loved to use this assessment. The parent interview really allows you to get great information about how the child is currently communicating.

Early Start Denver Model (ESDM) Checklist

- Evaluates skills across multiple domains:
  - Receptive communication
  - Expressive communication
  - Joint attention
  - Fine motor
  - Gross motor
  - Social skills
- Developed by Sally Rogers, PhD, and Geraldine Dawson, PhD
- Provides a curriculum-based assessment that directly informs intervention

I discuss the ESDM in our ASHA and ACE-approved course called Start Communicating Today. I love the specific skills that they outline in this tool. When we are working with younger learners, we really need to break the larger skills down, and this tool does that perfectly!

Verbal Behavior Milestones Assessment and Placement Program (VB-MAPP)

The VB-MAPP is used to determine a child's skills and barriers to design an individual program for each student. It contains 165 verbal behavior milestones across 16 different verbal operants and related skills and 3 developmental levels:

- Level 1: 0–18 months
- Level 2: 18–30 months
- Level 3: 30–48 months

- Developed by Mark Sundberg, PhD, BCBA-D
- Includes the Early Echoic Skills Assessment (EESA) developed by Dr. Barbara Esch
- Features a barriers assessment to identify obstacles to learning
- Provides a transition assessment to guide educational placement decisions
- Evaluates skills including requesting, labeling, receptive language, matching, play, social behavior, intraverbals, group skills, and more

The VB-MAPP is a common assessment tool given by BCBAs. If you are an SLP in a very specialized program, you may be more familiar with this tool. Not all SLPs feel comfortable administering this assessment, but if your student has been given this, it can provide a wealth of communication-based information that you can incorporate into your part of the assessment report.

Informal Observation and Parent Input

Now that we have discussed some of my favorite evaluation tools, I want to discuss other ways that we can get invaluable information. We will discuss parent input and observations.

Parent input is essential! I know as a speech therapist it can be hard to know exactly what questions to ask parents. I created a 20-question guide below that you can use in your next evaluation, which is included in the back of the book as Appendix B.

These questions will help you build a comprehensive understanding of the child's current communication profile, strengths, challenges, and the family's priorities, providing a foundation for developing an effective intervention plan.

For young autistic children who are just beginning to communicate, parent reports are particularly valuable. Parents often notice subtle communication attempts that may not be evident during a clinical assessment session.

Direct Observation

Observation is a critical component of a gold-standard assessment. It allows clinicians to:

- Observe communication forms and functions in natural contexts.
- Evaluate performance across different environments (classroom, playground, lunchroom, etc.).
- Assess interactions with different communication partners.
- Identify environmental factors that support or hinder communication.

When assessing toddlers and preschoolers, observation during play is especially informative. Watching how a child interacts with toys, peers, and adults provides valuable information about their communication abilities and preferences.

When assessing school-age students, I try to observe during a variety of times throughout the day. Observing a student during a structured group activity, during a specials class (music, art, gym), during lunch and recess can give you a solid idea of how the student is communicating across their day.

Informal Measures

When I was putting together Start Communicating and The Advanced Language Learner in the ABA Speech Connection, I knew that I wanted to share the informal measures that have helped me on my assessment journey. There will be times when you need to use more of an informal measure to assess your students. It may be that your current setting does not own the tools mentioned above or that your student did not participate in your structured assessment. Have no fear, I am including the informal assessments I have developed and shared inside the membership. I hope that these are helpful tools that you can start using now. These informal measures can be found in Appendix E: Informal Assessments.

Now that we have discussed the many different pieces and parts of an evaluation, let's look at some real-world case studies. I hope you see similarities in your caseload and that you can apply these soon.

CASE EXAMPLE: COLLABORATIVE ASSESSMENT

This case study illustrates a collaborative assessment approach. An early intervention-age preschool-age student was evaluated using a multidisciplinary team approach. The assessment components included:

- VB-MAPP administered by a consulting BCBA
- Academic testing completed by the classroom teacher

- Rossetti administered by the SLP
- Use of informal assessment by the SLP
- Parent input form
- Record review by all team members
- Direct observation across multiple settings

This comprehensive evaluation provided a complete picture of the student's strengths and needs. It allowed us to set functional goals for our student.

A school-age student was evaluated using a multidisciplinary team approach. The assessment components included:

- VB-MAPP administered by a consulting BCBA
- Functional behavior assessment (FBA) conducted by the BCBA to address behavioral barriers to learning
- Academic testing completed by the classroom teacher
- Parent input form
- Expressive One-Word Vocabulary Test administered by the SLP
- Receptive One-Word Vocabulary Test administered by the SLP
- Record review by all team members
- Direct observation across multiple settings

This comprehensive evaluation provided a complete picture of the student's strengths and needs, allowing the team to develop a targeted intervention plan addressing communication, behavior, and academic skills.

SUMMARY

A comprehensive assessment for autistic learners requires collaboration across disciplines, multiple assessment methods, and consideration of the individual's unique profile. Key takeaways include:

1. Collaborative assessment is essential for developing a holistic understanding of the autistic learner's strengths and needs.
2. Assessment should include standardized tests, criterion-referenced measures, interviews, observations, and informal measures.
3. Different assessment tools are appropriate for different age groups and developmental levels.

By adopting a comprehensive, collaborative approach to assessment, professionals can gather the information needed to design interventions that meaningfully improve communication skills and reduce behavioral barriers to learning for autistic individuals across the lifespan.

NOTES

1. Gerenser, J. E., & Koenig, M. A. (Eds.). (2019). *ABA for SLPs: Interprofessional collaboration for autism support teams*. Paul H. Brookes Publishing Co.

2. Wiig, E. H., Semel, E., & Secord, W. A. (2013). *Clinical Evaluation of Language Fundamentals– Fifth Edition (CELF-5)*. San Antonio, TX: Pearson.

3. Brownell, R. (2010). *Expressive One-Word Picture Vocabulary Tests Fourth Edition: Manual*. Pearson.

4. *Receptive One-Word Picture Vocabulary Test, Fourth Edition (ROWPVT-4)*. Academic Communication Associates.

5. Fudala, J. B., & Stegall, S. (2017). *Arizona-4: Arizona Articulation and Phonology Scale, Fourth Edition*. Western Psychological Services.

6. Rossetti, L. (2006). *The Rossetti infant-toddler language scale: A measure of communication and interaction*. East Moline, IL: LinguiSystems.

7. Rogers, S. J., & Dawson, G. (2009). *Early Start Denver Model Curriculum Checklist for Young Children with Autism*. Guilford Press.

8. Sundberg, M. L. (2008). *The Verbal Behavior Milestones Assessment and Placement Program: The VB MAPP*. Concord, CA: AVB Press.

9. Partington, J. W., & Mueller, M. M. (2016). *Assessment of Functional Living Skills Guide* (1.2 ed.). Partington Behavior Analysts.

10. McGreevy, P., Fry, T., & Cornwall, C. (2014). *Essential for Living* (2nd ed.). Orlando, FL: Patrick McGreevy, PhD, P.A. & Associates.

11. Rowland, C. (2004, 2011). *Communication Matrix*. Retrieved January 2, 2026, from www.communicationmatrix.org.

12. Kleiman, L. I. (2003). *Functional Communication Profile – Revised*. LinguiSystems.

CHAPTER 2

Beyond the Therapy Room: Teaching Skills That Generalize

It's difficult to convey just how much I hate butterscotch. When I was four, I was at a parade with my parents and the people in the parade were throwing out FREE candy! I ate a butterscotch and swallowed it. It got lodged in my throat—*fun times!* So, for me, butterscotch is the absolute worst. I go to get some candy during that 3 p.m. lull at a conference and all that they have left is butterscotch. Great, what am I going to do with this? I bring this up because in therapy, 100% of the clinician-focused therapy activities are the butterscotch. So in this chapter and book we are not talking about the butterscotch of the therapy world—we are talking about the chocolate! We are talking about naturalistic and more child-led activities.

A FOCUS ON NATURALISTIC INTERVENTION

For decades, the fields of speech-language pathology and applied behavior analysis have approached autism intervention from parallel paths with different philosophical foundations. Today, we are witnessing a meaningful convergence of these approaches through Naturalistic Developmental Behavioral Interventions (NDBIs).[1] This chapter explores the core principles of NDBIs and how practitioners across disciplines can implement these evidence-based strategies to support autistic learners in developing communication skills in authentic contexts.

As intervention approaches for autistic children have evolved, there has been a significant shift toward providing more naturalistic interventions that honor child-led therapy while maintaining scientific rigor. This shift represents not just a change in technique but a fundamental shift of how we view effective learning environments for autistic individuals.

NDBIs are a scientifically validated set of interventions derived primarily from the fields of applied behavior analysis (ABA) and developmental psychology. What distinguishes a true NDBI from other intervention approaches is the presence of several key elements:

- An intervention manual with clear protocols
- Procedures for treatment fidelity
- Ongoing measurement of progress
- Evidence-based practices supported by empirical research

Prominent examples of comprehensive NDBIs include:

- Early Start Denver Model (ESDM)
- Enhanced Milieu Teaching
- Walden Toddler Program
- JASPER (Joint Attention, Symbolic Play, Engagement, and Regulation)
- Pivotal Response Treatment (PRT)
- Project ImPACT

While each of these programs has specific protocols and training requirements, they share core elements that can be integrated into everyday practice by speech-language pathologists, behavior analysts, teachers, and parents.[2]

AWAY FROM THE TABLE

I will never forget when I started to make a shift from more tabletop tasks to a more naturalistic approach to intervention. It was very early in my career, and I was working with an autistic student in his home. He was three years old and full of energy! He was not the kind of student who would sit at a table for more than 30 seconds. I knew that I needed to try something different.

Instead of focusing on tasks where he needed to sit for extended periods of time, I set up his sessions so that they were child-led but semistructured. We began each session with work on joint attention skills. This is where I developed my three-pronged approach to working on joint attention (Chapter 3) but in short, I used books, music, and play as the foundation for my therapy sessions.

My client would greet me at the door. And our first activity was music! I always tried to pick songs that have motions, like "Wheels on the Bus" and "If You're Happy and You Know It." Songs like this are great because if my client didn't feel like singing along, he could participate by doing some of the motions. Next was a play activity. One of our favorite activities was a play sequence where we each had a baby doll. We would feed the babies, burp the babies, and then put them to bed. The next activity included a book. One of his favorite books was more of a book/song combo called *Pete the Cat: I Love My White Shoes* by Eric Litman. I love this book and any book in this series because it has book and song qualities.

Shifting from tabletop and adult-directed tasks to a more natural, child-centered framework helped him not only thrive but start communicating on his own for the first time. And we were both having fun!

I will offer examples that can be used in 1:1 or 1:2 therapy sessions. If you are seeing students in a group setting, I will cover group therapy extensively in Chapter 7. As a school-based therapist with over 20 years of experience, I can't wait to share tips and strategies for setting up group therapy that is fun and functional.

We'll explore the science behind the naturalistic approach. And if you are already using a more naturalistic approach, hopefully this information will build on your body of knowledge and give you confidence in why NDBI is essential for our students/clients.

Before exploring the components of naturalistic interventions, it's important to understand why highly structured, clinician-directed approaches often fall short despite their apparent efficiency. Research has identified several limitations to exclusively table-based, adult-directed intervention:

1. **Poor generalization:** Skills learned in highly structured contexts often fail to generalize across settings, people, and materials.
2. **Increased escape-avoidance behaviors:** When instruction is exclusively adult-directed, children may develop challenging behaviors to escape demands.
3. **Lack of spontancity:** Highly prompted environments can create response patterns that depend on adult cues rather than natural opportunities.
4. **Prompt dependence:** Children may become overly reliant on adult prompts rather than responding to natural cues in the environment.

While structured teaching certainly has its place in a comprehensive intervention program, these limitations highlight the need for balancing structure with naturalistic approaches that prompt independent communication and foster generalization.

CORE ELEMENTS OF NATURALISTIC INTERVENTIONS

There are three core elements of naturalistic interventions:

1. Engagement, affect, and shared enjoyment
2. Context of treatment delivery
3. Instructional strategies

Engagement, Affect, and Shared Enjoyment

At the heart of effective naturalistic intervention is the quality of social engagement between the therapist and child. NDBI approaches emphasize:

- **Positive, warm affect:** The extent to which practitioners convey positive emotion such as happiness, joy, interest, and alertness
- **Shared enjoyment:** Engaging in social interaction for the mere pleasure of connecting with another person
- **Heightened animation:** Using animated facial expressions, varied tone of voice, and enthusiastic responses to maintain engagement
- **Matching affect to the child's state:** Being responsive to the child's emotional needs and adjusting your communication style accordingly

Research demonstrates that learning is enhanced when it occurs within emotionally meaningful social interactions. When instruction is delivered without emotional engagement, the quality of learning suffers significantly.

Context of Treatment Delivery

Where and how intervention occurs matters tremendously. Rather than conducting all instruction at a table with flashcards, naturalistic approaches embed learning opportunities within:

- Play-based activities that follow the child's interests
- Daily routines such as snack time, arrival, and transitions
- Sensory-rich experiences that are motivating and fun
- Community settings where skills will naturally be used

Consider the difference between these two approaches to teaching labeling:

- **Traditional approach:** Child sits at the table while adult holds up pictures and says, "What is it?"
- **Naturalistic approach:** During play with a farm-themed sensory bin, therapist and child take turns finding animals, naming them, and creating a story about them.

Both approaches target labeling, but the naturalistic context increases motivation and makes the skill immediately functional and a whole lot more fun!

Instructional Strategies

Environmental Arrangement

Environmental arrangement involves structuring the physical space and materials to create natural opportunities for communication and learning. Key strategies include:

- **Controlling access:** Placing desired items in sight but out of reach (on a high shelf) or in clear containers that require assistance to open. We may have items visible that the student loves and enjoys but they are out of reach. This would be a great way to set up the environment to work on pointing to a preferred item or verbalizing too.
- **Assistance:** Introducing materials that require help to operate. You could have a super fun toy, but it is in a clear container that is hard to open. This is the perfect opportunity to practice "help."
- **Expectant waiting:** Looking at the child with an expectant expression, waiting for communication. I love to use this strategy with bubbles. I pull out the bubbles. "Okay, we are going to blow bubbles." I blow bubbles, pop some bubbles, and then when they are gone, I wait to see if the student wants more bubbles.
- **Violating routines:** Changing familiar sequences to prompt the child to notice and respond. An example of this would be to put your shoe on first and then your sock. Little ones think things like this are hilarious and they love to correct you!

These arrangements create authentic reasons for children to communicate without artificial prompting.

Natural Reinforcement

Reinforcement refers to the strengthening of a behavior and making that behavior more likely to occur because of what happens immediately following that behavior.

Natural reinforcement involves providing consequences that are directly related to the child's response:

- **Natural reinforcer:** If a child says "car," they get to play with the car.
- **Indirect/unrelated reinforcer:** If a child says "car," they receive a token or edible.

While unrelated reinforcers may sometimes be necessary to establish initial responding, naturalistic interventions emphasize planning for systematic fading toward natural reinforcement. Natural reinforcement helps children understand the functional value of communication and increases the likelihood that skills will generalize beyond the therapy setting.

Maintenance Tasks

Effective intervention balances new learning with previously mastered skills. Including maintenance tasks (easy tasks), which are skills that the child can already do:

- Keeps overall reinforcement high
- Builds behavioral momentum
- Creates a positive learning experience
- Prevents skill regression

An effective rhythm might include: easy skill, easy skill, challenging skill, easy skill—much like a well-designed exercise program that alternates between manageable and challenging activities.

In therapy, this might look like the following:

SLP: Has a toy ball and says "ball" (easy)

Client: "ball"

SLP: "Let's say hi to Mr. Teddy Bear." *holds up teddy bear*

Client: "Hi Teddy." (easy)

SLP: "Mr. Bear is so hungry." *feeds Mr. Bear a cookie*; "you try" (hard)

Client: "cookie" *feeds Mr. Bear a cookie*

Prompting and Modeling

Prompting can be defined as a cue between the instruction and the target behavior being taught.

Modeling refers to a teaching procedure where the clinician demonstrates a target behavior or skill for the purpose of having the learner observe and subsequently imitate or learn from that demonstration.

Naturalistic approaches use prompts as teaching tools, not mere compliance mechanisms. Effective prompting includes:

- Visual supports embedded within activities
- Models that demonstrate the target skill
- Time delay to allow for independent responding
- Following the child's attention focus when introducing prompts

Balanced Turns

Social reciprocity develops through balanced turn-taking during activities. This back-and-forth exchange:

- Teaches the rhythm of communication
- Creates multiple opportunities for modeling and practice
- Builds social engagement
- Establishes a foundation for conversation

Modified games like simplified Connect Four provide structured opportunities to practice turn-taking without the cognitive load of complex rules. We will talk about a variety of modified leisure skills in Chapter 4 when we get into social skills and play.

Child Imitation and Adult Imitation

While traditional approaches focus on having the child imitate the adult, reciprocal imitation training also includes strategic adult imitation of appropriate child actions. Research indicates that when adults imitate children's actions, children become more socially attentive and engage in increased social behaviors.

Multiple Examples

Using varied materials and examples helps children develop broader conceptual understanding rather than narrow stimulus-response patterns. For example, when teaching the concept "cookie," using different types, sizes, and representations of cookies helps the child understand the concept beyond a single example. When we plan therapy to include multiple examples, we are helping our student generalize these skills from the therapeutic environment to the everyday environment.

Child-initiated Teaching Episodes

Perhaps the most challenging yet valuable component of naturalistic intervention is following the child's lead. This doesn't mean abandoning all structure, but rather:

- Observing what captures the child's interest
- Joining their activity without disrupting their engagement
- Introducing teaching opportunities within their chosen activity
- Expanding on their communication attempts

This delicate balance of child-led activity with adult-guided learning requires practice and flexibility but leads to greater engagement and more meaningful learning. I feel like speech therapy is like a mixture of science and art. A well-run naturalistic therapy session is like a dance! Sometimes the child is leading and sometimes the clinician is leading. If child-led activities make you a bit nervous—start with sensory social routines. They are more child-led but give us a general structure.

SENSORY SOCIAL ROUTINES

Sensory social routines are back-and-forth ritualized social exchanges that are highly reinforcing for both the adult and child. These routines:

- Incorporate movement, sound, and tactile experiences
- Include predictable yet variable elements
- Create shared joy
- Provide foundations for turn-taking and social engagement

Effective sensory social routines for young children include:

1. **"The Achoo! Game":** Place a block on your head, pretending to sneeze ("achoo!"), and letting it fall off—then waiting for the child to retrieve it and give it back. This is an amazing way to naturally work on eye gaze and social engagement.
2. **"That's Yucky!":** Make exaggerated, disgusted faces while feeding a stuffed animal pretend food, encouraging the child to join in the game. Think toy broccoli and onions!
3. **"Boo-Boo":** Create a pretend scenario where toys need bandages, building early empathy and caretaking scripts. The word Boo-Boo also contains the *b* sound, which is an early developing sound. This can make for a great naturalistic verbal imitation target.
4. **"Here Comes the Car":** Use toy vehicles with different sounds and movements, encouraging the child to request different cars or actions. For example, the blue truck has a deep loud voice and the tiny red car has a soft high voice.
5. **"Time for Baby":** Use baby dolls to create predictable caregiving routines like feeding, burping, and putting to sleep. Make sure to have two sets for this activity. Taking turns with materials can be difficult for emerging communicators, so having two sets allows us to each have our own and model, too!

These routines can be integrated into a session framework that might include:

- Opening with music and movement
- Transitioning to a sensory social routine
- Incorporating a literacy-based activity

IMPLEMENTING NATURALISTIC STRATEGIES

Shifting to a more naturalistic approach doesn't mean abandoning structure entirely. Instead, consider these implementation guidelines:

1. **Start with observation:** Before diving into teaching, spend time observing what naturally motivates and engages the child.
2. **Create an engaging environment:** Set up the physical space with high-interest materials that encourage interaction.
3. **Follow the child's lead:** Use their interests as entry points for teaching rather than redirecting to your agenda.
4. **Build in structured opportunities:** Plan activities that naturally create opportunities for practicing target skills.
5. **Respond contingently:** When the child communicates, respond immediately and naturally to reinforce the attempt.
6. **Track progress:** Even in naturalistic contexts, systematic data collection remains important for measuring growth.

I know that this can all seem a bit overwhelming at first. I like to use the following questions to gauge whether my sessions are more naturalistic in nature. You don't have to answer all these perfectly, by any stretch! This just gives you a baseline for your journey toward providing more naturalistic therapy.

1. How do I follow the child's lead and interests rather than solely imposing my own agenda?
2. How do my sessions incorporate play-based activities that are motivating to the child?
3. How am I creating genuine reasons for communication rather than artificial "say this" prompts?
4. How have I arranged the environment to naturally encourage communication attempts?
5. In what ways do I show genuine enthusiasm and warmth during our interactions?
6. Am I using natural reinforcers that directly relate to what the child is communicating about?
7. Do I balance structured activities with child-initiated learning opportunities?
8. Do I wait expectantly for the child to initiate communication?
9. How do I embed learning opportunities within meaningful everyday contexts?
10. In what ways do I move beyond the therapy table to utilize the entire environment?
11. What sensory-social routines do I use that promote back-and-forth interaction?
12. Am I using multiple examples of vocabulary concepts to promote generalization?

13. Have I reduced my reliance on artificial reinforcers (tokens, stickers) in favor of natural consequences?

14. Am I promoting balanced turns rather than directing all the interactions?

15. How often do I imitate the child's appropriate actions to increase their social attention?

16. How do I consider the child's emotional state and adjust my approach accordingly?

17. Have I created opportunities for spontaneous communication rather than just prompted responses?

18. How do I incorporate movement and sensory experiences that engage the whole child?

19. How do I use literacy and music in ways that encourage active participation rather than passive listening?

20. Am I collecting data on spontaneous communication in addition to prompted responses?

These questions can help therapists reflect on whether they're truly implementing the principles of naturalistic developmental behavioral interventions in their practice.

CASE EXAMPLES: THERAPY SESSION USING NATURALISTIC STRATEGIES

- Opening with music and movement: "Wheels on the Bus"
- Transitioning to a sensory social routine: "The Achoo! Game"
- Incorporating a literacy-based activity: *Pete the Cat and His White Shoes*
- Opening with music and movement: "Old MacDonald Had a Farm"
- Transitioning to a sensory social routine: "That's Yucky!"
- Incorporating a literacy-based activity: *Chicka Chicka Boom Boom*
- Opening with music and movement: "If You're Happy and You Know It"
- Transitioning to a sensory social routine: "Boo Boo"
- Incorporating a literacy-based activity: *Brown Bear, Brown Bear*
- Opening with music and movement: "The Alphabet Song"
- Transitioning to a sensory social routine: "Here Comes the Car"
- Incorporating a literacy-based activity: *I Went Walking*
- Opening with music and movement: "5 Little Monkeys Jumping on the Bed"
- Transitioning to a sensory social routine: "Time for Baby"
- Incorporating a literacy-based activity: *Huggy Kissy*

CONCLUSION

NDBIs represent an exciting convergence of developmental and behavioral approaches to supporting autistic learners. By embedding learning opportunities within meaningful social contexts, following the child's lead, and emphasizing shared enjoyment, practitioners can foster communication development that generalizes across settings and partners.

As you implement these strategies, remember that the shift to naturalistic intervention is often as much about changing our mindset as changing our techniques. By viewing therapy as a dance between scientific principles and authentic human connection, we can create learning experiences that are both effective and joyful—the chocolate of the therapy world rather than the butterscotch.

NOTES

1. Bruinsma, Y., Minjarez, M. B., Schreibman, L., & Stahmer, A. C. (Eds.). (2020). *Naturalistic Developmental Behavioral Interventions for Autism Spectrum Disorder*. Paul H. Brookes Publishing Co.
2. Schreibman, L., Dawson, G., Stahmer, A. C., Landa, R., Rogers, S. J., McGee, G. G., ... & Halladay, A. (2015). Naturalistic developmental behavioral interventions: Empirically validated treatments for autism spectrum disorder. *Journal of Autism and Developmental Disorders, 45*(8), 2411–2428.

CHAPTER 3

When Your Student Won't Engage: Strategies to Build Social Connection

I checked my notes one last time before pulling into the quiet suburban neighborhood. This would be my first session with Adam, a three-year-old recently diagnosed with autism. His parents had been thrilled to discover that I lived just five minutes away—a small miracle in the world of specialized therapy where families often traveled hours for appointments.

As I rang the doorbell, I mentally reviewed my toolkit of bubbles, animal toys, and songs. Adam's mother greeted me with a warm smile and ushered me inside. In the living room, Adam clutched a toy car, moving it back and forth and didn't look up when I entered the room.

"He's not talking yet," his mother explained, "We're really concerned about him."

I began unpacking my materials. Most children loved bubbles, so that's what I started with, but Adam didn't even glance my way as I opened the container.

So, I switched strategies. I arranged farm animals on the floor and began singing "Old McDonald" in my cringe-worthy voice. Adam approached for about 15 seconds, just long enough to grab the plastic pig, before returning to his solitary play.

By our fourth session, Adam's parents asked the question that had clearly been weighing on them: "When will you work on him talking?" They seemed concerned about my focus on shared activities and joint attention rather than flashcard drills to prompt verbal speech.

Drawing on my years of experience, I gently explained the importance of building connection first. I knew that first words emerged not from rote memorization but from meaningful moments of engagement. Each session, I measured small victories—Adam staying engaged for 15 seconds, then 30, then 45 seconds.

During our fifth session, I brought something special—a bag containing tiny objects. I shook a small shoe inside a brown bag, making an intriguing sound.

"I have a toy for you," I told Adam. "No peeking!"

Adam was curious, he approached and reached his little hand inside. When he pulled out the miniature shoe, something magical happened.

"Shoe," he said clearly.

The room seemed to freeze in that perfect moment. "Wow, Adam!" I exclaimed. "I love hearing your voice, it is a shoe!"

His mom rushed over, giving him a bear hug. Adam smiled—he had done it. He had said his first word. The shared joy between therapist, parent, and child was amazing, a celebration of connection that had blossomed from those early moments of joint attention.

In that breakthrough, I was reminded why I had chosen this profession. The journey to helping children find their voice was often slow and required patience, but moments like these—witnessing a child begin their communication journey—made it all worthwhile.

For Adam, it was just the beginning. For me, it was confirmation of what I had always known: *building connection comes first, and communication will follow.*

Adam's growth trajectory led me to develop the **Connect and Engage Approach**. This is a three-pronged approach where we use books, music, and play to build the foundation for increased connection, joint attention, and communication. More about that in a bit.

This chapter explores the foundations of joint attention, its typical developmental course, assessment approaches, evidence-based intervention, and the Connect and Engage Approach. By understanding the intricate relationship between joint attention, social engagement, and language development, speech-language pathologists can design comprehensive interventions that address the foundational social-cognitive skills that underlie communication.

JOINT ATTENTION

Communication begins long before students say their first word. Joint attention serves as a crucial milestone that creates a bridge between early social experiences and later language development. For speech-language pathologists working with diverse populations, understanding the mechanisms, development, and clinical applications of joint attention is essential for effective assessment and intervention.

Joint attention refers to the shared focus of two individuals on an object or event, accompanied by a mutual awareness that they are both attending to the same thing. This seemingly simple ability represents a complex integration of social, cognitive, and attentional skills that emerge during infancy and continue to develop through early childhood. For typically developing children, joint attention unfolds naturally through everyday interactions. However, for autistic children, the development of joint attention often follows a different trajectory. Due to this, speech-language pathologists should understand joint attention and how it can be embedded into therapy sessions.

Joint attention can happen all around us. For example, when a child points to an airplane, alternates their gaze between the adult and airplane, and makes a verbal comment, they are initiating joint attention. When the adult responds by looking at the airplane and commenting, they complete this social exchange.

From a behavioral perspective, joint attention can be characterized by both its response class (the behaviors involved) and its function (the purpose it serves). Dube et al. (2004) conceptualize joint attention as a response class that includes orienting, pointing, and vocal commenting, maintained by socially mediated reinforcement. This means that the social consequences provided by others (e.g., shared attention, social connection) serve as the reinforcers that maintain joint attention behaviors.[1]

Joint attention is commonly divided into two main categories:

1. **Responding to joint attention (RJA).** This involves following another person's bid for attention, such as following a point or gaze shift to share a focus of attention. For example, when an adult points to a bird in the sky, a child demonstrates RJA by looking in the direction of the point.
2. **Initiating joint attention (IJA).** This involves spontaneously directing another person's attention to an object or event of interest.[2]

This distinction is important because research suggests these behaviors may represent distinct skills with different developmental trajectories and relationships to later language and social development.

The development of joint attention begins in the first months of life with basic orienting responses to social stimuli. By 3–4 months, infants show a preference for human faces and engage in dyadic (person-to-person) interactions through mutual gaze and affective exchanges. Between 6–9 months, infants begin to coordinate their attention between people and objects, marking the transition from dyadic to triadic (person-object-person) interactions. Around 8–10 months, most infants begin responding to joint attention bids by following the direction of an adult's gaze or point. By 9–12 months, infants start to actively direct others' attention through pointing, showing objects, and alternating gaze between objects and social partners. These early joint attention behaviors represent important precursors to intentional communication.

According to research, the development of more coordinated joint attention typically occurs around 18 months in typically developing children. At this stage, a child who points to a preferred object while shifting gaze between the object and their social partner is exhibiting this form of joint attention.

As children progress through the toddler and preschool years, joint attention becomes increasingly sophisticated and integrated with language and play. By two years old, most children smoothly coordinate attention with others across various contexts and can maintain joint engagement for extended periods.

Between ages two and five, joint attention skills continue to develop in complexity, supporting more nuanced social interactions, collaborative play, and conversational exchanges.

During this period, children become more adept at following complex verbal directions about objects outside their immediate visual field and use increasingly sophisticated linguistic means to direct others' attention.

The relationship between joint attention and language development is robust and well-documented.

Research indicates that *early joint attention skills predict later language development,* even when controlling for initial language levels. Specifically:

1. Responding to joint attention at 6–12 months predicts receptive language development at 24–30 months.
2. Initiating joint attention, particularly high-level behaviors like pointing and showing, predicts expressive language development.
3. The duration and quality of joint engagement episodes correlate with vocabulary growth rates.

These associations highlight why joint attention is considered a pivotal skill for language acquisition—it creates the social-cognitive foundation upon which language is built.

One of the most consistent findings in autism research is that autistic learners show significant differences in joint attention development. These differences are often evident before formal diagnosis, typically appearing within the first year of life, and affect both responding to and initiating joint attention.

Autistic children may show:

- Decreased frequency of responding to bids for joint attention
- Reduced monitoring of others' attention
- Fewer spontaneous initiations of joint attention
- Greater impairment in high-level initiations (showing/pointing) than low-level initiations (gaze alternation)
- Relative preservation of pointing to request (protoimperative pointing) compared to pointing to share interest (protodeclarative pointing)

These patterns suggest that the social-motivational aspects of joint attention may be particularly affected in autism, while more instrumental functions remain more intact.

Joint attention deficits have significant implications for language development in autistic children. Research suggests that these early differences can impact at least four learning opportunities:

1. **Word learning opportunities.** Children may miss social cues.
2. **Pragmatic development.** Joint attention forms the foundation for understanding communicative intentions.

3. **Conversational abilities.** Difficulty coordinating attention affects turn-taking and topic maintenance.
4. **Narrative development.** This requires shared understanding and mutual focus.

Importantly, joint attention ability in young autistic children is one of the strongest predictors of language outcomes, highlighting its central role in communication development.

Naturalistic Observation

While structured assessments provide valuable standardized information, naturalistic observation is essential for understanding joint attention in everyday contexts:

1. **Parent–child interaction observations.** Observing how children respond to and initiate joint attention during play with caregivers provides ecologically valid information about these skills.
2. **Classroom observations.** For preschool and school-age children, observing joint attention during classroom activities can reveal how these skills manifest in educational settings.
3. **Peer interaction observations.** Assessing joint attention during interactions with peers can provide insight into how these skills function in more complex social contexts.

When assessing joint attention, speech-language pathologists should consider five factors:

1. **Range.** The full range of joint attention behaviors, including both responding to and initiating joint attention.
2. **Contexts.** Performance can vary across settings and partners, so the contexts in which joint attention is observed are important.
3. **Aspects.** Motivational aspects affective assessment, as interest in materials can significantly affect joint attention.
4. **Variations.** Cultural variations in joint attention expressions affect assessment, as cultural practices may influence how these skills develop and are expressed.
5. **Integration.** The integration of standardized assessment and naturalistic observation will affect a comprehensive understanding of strengths and needs.

This multifaceted assessment approach provides the foundation for targeted intervention planning.

For speech-language pathologists working with young children, joint attention should be considered a foundational element of intervention, not an optional add-on.

Strategies for Integration

1. Begin sessions with child-led play that emphasizes mutual engagement before introducing more structured activities.
2. Use environmental arrangement to create opportunities for joint attention (e.g., placing interesting items on high shelves, introducing novel or unexpected elements).
3. Embed joint attention goals within naturalistic language intervention approaches.
4. Follow a developmental sequence, targeting responding to joint attention before more complex initiating behaviors.
5. Use visual supports and props that are highly motivating to support joint attention development.

The goal is not to teach joint attention in isolation but to weave it into the fabric of comprehensive communication intervention.

Different strategies may be appropriate depending on a child's current joint attention skills:

For children who rarely engage in joint attention:

- Begin with highly engaging sensory-social routines (e.g., peek-a-boo, tickle games).
- Use animated facial expressions and exaggerated prosody to increase social salience.
- Follow the child's attentional focus rather than redirecting it.
- Provide immediate natural consequences for any joint attention behavior.

For children who respond to but rarely initiate joint attention:

- Create situations that naturally elicit comment (e.g., unexpected events, novel toys).
- Model pointing and commenting frequently.
- Use environmental arrangement to encourage initiations (e.g., wind-up toys that stop).
- Reinforce spontaneous initiations with enthusiastic social responses.

For children who initiate primarily to request:

- Shift the function of existing behaviors (e.g., from requesting to commenting).
- Emphasize the social reward aspect of sharing experiences.
- Create routines where commenting receives as much reinforcement as requesting.
- Gradually increase the social demands of interactions.

THE CONNECT AND ENGAGE APPROACH

I created this three-pronged approach that guides my therapy for students who are not yet speaking. I know the overwhelm when you feel like your students are not making progress despite your best efforts! I hated that feeling and that motivated me to really dig into the research on joint attention. Creating this research-supported approach has helped me feel more confident, and I know that it will help you feel that way too.

I will introduce each section of the Connect and Engage Approach with a goal. This is a goal from the Autism IEP Goal bank that I will share within the book. After the goal I will share how I set up activities within the therapy sessions.

Books

GOAL: Student will engage in a shared interaction with the therapist while engaged in a literacy-based activity for a duration of three minutes without prompts, over three consecutive sessions.

We know that literacy-based activities are important to embed in therapy, but how do we even get started? I have a couple of rules that I always live by.

Tips for Getting Started

1. **Present a book** that you think your student may enjoy or give them a choice of two books (choosing increases motivation within sessions).
2. **Use your own voice** when reading the book. (This is essential for social engagement.)
3. **Make it fun.** Don't force engagement. If your student gets up after 30 seconds, just mark that on the data sheet. Keep reading and using an excited tone of voice. They may come back to see what you are doing.
4. **Use the same book for three sessions.** This is not from a research article, but just from my lived experience as a therapist. Session 1 allows you to introduce the book. Session 2 allows your student to participate a bit and session 3 will allow your student to participate with an activity that feels more familiar.

Books I Love to Use for This Age Group

1. *Pete the Cat and His White Shoes*[3]
2. *Brown Bear, Brown Bear*[4]
3. *Huggy Kissy*[5]
4. *Good Night, Gorilla*[6]
5. *Llama Llama Red Pajama*[7]
6. *Pete the Cat Perfect Pizza Party*[8]
7. *If You Give a Mouse a Cookie*[9]
8. *Splat the Cat*[10]
9. *I Went Walking*[11]
10. *If You Give a Dog a Donut*[12]

Music

GOAL: Student will engage in a shared interaction with the therapist while engaged in a music-based activity for a duration of three minutes without prompts, over two consecutive sessions.

We know that music-based activities are a great way to focus on connection, communication, and movement! I have a couple of tips when using music in therapy.

Tips for Incorporating Music

1. Pick songs that have motions. This helps with practicing imitation and allows a student who is not yet speaking to participate.
2. Use visuals. This can be a fun way to engage students. I have an early intervention song guide available at www.abaspeech.org.
3. **Have fun!** See how this is a recurring theme? Sing the song, be silly, and encourage engagement.

Songs I Love to Use for This Age Group

1. "Wheels on the Bus"
2. "Head, Shoulders, Knees, and Toes"
3. "If You're Happy and You Know It"
4. "5 Little Monkeys"
5. "The Alphabet Song"

An early intervention song guide I created for Old MacDonald.

Play

GOAL: Student will engage in a shared interaction with the therapist while engaging in a cooperative activity with the therapist for a duration of three minutes without prompts, over three consecutive sessions.

We know that play-based activities are a great way to focus on connection and communication. I have found over the years that many of my students have trouble engaging in traditional cooperative play activities. So below I will share a variety of fun and cooperative activities that can be used in sessions to work on joint attention skills.

Activity 1: What Is in the Bag?

1. Grab a small bag that you can't see through.
2. Grab some mini objects.
3. Don't let your student see but put one item in the bag.
4. Shake the bag and say some variation of "Shake, shake, shake" to naturally get your learner's attention.
5. Ask, "What is in the bag? Come and see."
6. Have them pick the object out of the bag. Label the item if your student is not yet working on this skill.
7. Repeat with a variety of objects.

Activity 2: Mailbox Time

1. Grab 5–10 flashcard pictures.
2. Grab a mini mailbox toy or just a box with a hole/slot in the top. Make sure that it is large enough to place the flashcard. A Kleenex box might also work here.[13]
3. Spread out the cards face down on the table.
4. Explain the game: "Okay, we are going to grab a picture and put it in the box."
5. Take the first turn. Turn over a card, label the card, and put it into the box.
6. Have your student do the rest of the cards or alternate turns with you.

Activity 3: Mini Basketball Game

1. Grab a mini basketball hoop or mini basketball organizer.
2. Have 5–10 mini balls.
3. Explain the game: "We are going to play basketball."
4. Take the first turn. Pick up a ball, stand close to the basket, and toss it in.
5. Take turns with your student tossing the rest of the balls into the basket.

Activity 4: The Egg Carton Game

1. Get an egg carton.
2. Put a mini object into each section of the egg carton.
3. Explain the game: "We are going to see what is inside."
4. Take the first turn. Pick one item up, show your student, and label the item.
5. Take turns with your student or have them take each item out. Practice showing the items and labeling, too. If your student is not yet working on labeling, label the item for them.

Activity 5: Feed the Animals

1. Grab 5–10 mini stuffed animals and play food items.
2. Explain the activity: "We are going to feed the animals."
3. Pull out each animal and label it and/or say *hello* ("Hello doggie").
4. Have your student line up the animals.
5. Pick up one animal and pretend that they are whispering to you, "I am hungry." Tell your student "Oh the (animal) is hungry! Let's feed them."
6. Grab a piece of play food and tell your student, for example, "We better feed the dog. Here is a biscuit."
7. Take the first turn and feed an animal.
8. Take turns until all the animals are "fed."

Now that you feel ready to implement the connect and engage approach to your next session, let's explore collaboration!

Collaborative Intervention with Other Professionals

Joint attention intervention is most effective when implemented collaboratively across contexts:

1. **Coordination with occupational therapists.** Address sensory regulation issues that may impact joint attention and incorporate joint attention goals into sensory-motor activities.
2. **Collaboration with behavioral therapists.** Ensure consistency in joint attention teaching strategies and reinforcement approaches across therapeutic contexts.
3. **Partnership with early childhood educators.** Support the generalization of joint attention skills to classroom settings through environmental modifications and teacher training.

4. **Team-based goal setting.** Develop interdisciplinary goals for joint attention that can be addressed across therapeutic contexts and home environments.

This collaborative approach increases the consistency and intensity of intervention, promoting more rapid skill development and generalization.

CASE STUDY EXAMPLES

Case Study 1: Early Intervention for a Toddler with Language Delay

Background: Maya, a 22-month-old girl with a significant expressive language delay, was referred for early intervention services. Assessment revealed age-appropriate receptive language but only five spoken words. Observation indicated limited joint attention initiations, though she would follow points and gaze shifts inconsistently.

Intervention approach: The speech-language pathologist implemented a developmental approach focused on building joint engagement during play:

1. Following Maya's lead and joining her play activities
2. Implementing the connect and engage approach by using books, music, and play in therapy
3. Creating playful routines with clear turns that encouraged gaze alternation
4. Using environmental arrangement (e.g., placing toys in clear containers) to create opportunities for joint problem-solving
5. Coaching parents to respond enthusiastically to any joint attention behaviors

Outcomes: After 12 weeks of twice-weekly sessions and consistent parent implementation, Maya showed significant increases in:

- Duration of joint engagement episodes
- Frequency of gaze alternation between objects and people
- Use of pointing to direct attention
- Vocalization during joint attention episodes

These improvements coincided with a vocabulary burst, with Maya acquiring 25 new words during the intervention period. This case illustrates how targeting joint attention can catalyze language development for children with language delays.

CONCLUSION

For speech-language pathologists, joint attention represents a crucial area of expertise that bridges social, cognitive, and linguistic development. By recognizing the foundational role of joint attention in communication development and incorporating evidence-based strategies to assess and support these skills, we can provide more comprehensive and effective services to the populations we serve.

After you read this book and implement the connect and engage method of using books, music, and play in your sessions, please share with me! You can reach me at my site www.abaspeech.org or on Instagram @abaspeechbyrose.

Joint attention is more than just a developmental milestone—it is the gateway through which children enter the social world of shared meaning that makes human communication possible. As such, it deserves our continued attention as researchers, clinicians, and advocates for our students.

NOTES

1. Dube, W. V., MacDonald, R. P. F., Mansfield, R. C., Holcomb, W. L., & Ahearn, W. H. (2004). Toward a behavioral analysis of joint attention. *The Behavior Analyst, 27*(2), 197–207. https://doi.org/10.1007/BF03393180.

2. Mundy, P., & Newell, L. (2007). Attention, joint attention, and social cognition. *Current Directions in Psychological Science, 16*(5), 269–274. https://doi.org/10.1111/j.1467-8721.2007.00518.

3. Litwin, Eric, & Dean, J. (2010). *Pete the Cat: I Love My White Shoes.* HarperCollins.

4. Martin, B., & Carle, E. (2004). *Brown Bear, Brown Bear, What Do You See?* Henry Holt & Co.

5. Patricelli, L. (2012). *Huggy Kissy.* Candlewick Press.

6. Rathmann, P. (1994). *Good Night, Gorilla.* G.P. Putnam's Sons.

7. Dewdney, A. (2005). *Llama, Llama Red Pajama.* Viking.

8. Dean, K., & Dean, J. (2019). *Pete the Cat and the Perfect Pizza Party.* HarperCollins.

9. Numeroff, L. J., & Bond, F. (1985). *If You Give a Mouse a Cookie.* Harper & Row, Publishers.

10. Scotton, R., & Farley, R (2010). *Splat the Cat.* HarperCollins.

11. Williams, S., & Vivas, J. (1990). *I Went Walking.* Harcourt Brace Jovanovich.

12. Numeroff, L. J., & Bond, F. (2011). *If You Give a Dog a Donut.* Balzer + Bray.

13. This is a strategy discussed by my friend, Dr. Mary Barbera.

CHAPTER 4

Stop Forcing Turn-taking: Play-based Social Learning That Actually Works

I'll never forget meeting Grant. He was nine, autistic, and he had no way to communicate with the world. He had just transitioned from his public-school program to the specialized school that I was working in. I remember our first sessions. I had brought a lot of toys and play items I thought he would love. I tried to engage him with the light-up spikey ball, but he didn't even look up. I gave it some more thought, and then I got out the alligator toy that made noise when you moved it. Grant gave it and me a fleeting eye gaze, but that was about it.

I was feeling really defeated when session after session Grant did not engage with me or with any of the therapy activities I had planned. I was in a unique situation in that I saw Grant one hour during the week for therapy, and I also saw him one hour a week for outpatient therapy. I loved seeing him for outpatient therapy because I was able to build rapport with his mom. I would spend the last 10 minutes discussing the session with his mom. It was during these discussions that his mom shared that he loved looking at himself in the mirror. That made me remember a light-up vanity mirror that my sister used to have that had a magnifier and was bordered with lights. I reached out to our clinical team, and someone had an old mirror just like this. They brought it in for our next session, and Grant loved it! He sat down, looked at himself in the mirror, and smiled. It was amazing to see Grant light up—literally *and* figuratively!

So, what does this have to do with social skills and play? Well, it all starts with connection. I had to figure out a way to connect. After I found that connection, he started to engage a bit more. I also felt like 60 minutes was way too long for one session, so I broke those up into two 30-minute sessions. This change was perfect for him. He was happier to attend therapy and was more engaged in sessions. The mirror was present throughout our sessions, too. We would start with the mirror and other potentially preferred items. We would then work on some of these targeted goals (engaging in a turn-taking activity was one of them), and at the end of the session we did some more mirror time.

One of the turn-taking activities that we tried was a success, in that he loved it and required very minimal prompting to engage. The game that we played was modified Connect Four. Grant was pretty social; he tended to smile often when others were around. I remember that the first time I presented Connect Four, Grant seemed intrigued. I held up a yellow and red token and asked him what color he wanted to be. He pointed toward red. I handed him a red token and he put it right into the game board. I then put in a yellow. I put another red token by him—he picked it up and put it in the game. He was engaged and smiling! I felt a sigh of relief! It took a while to find something that Grant enjoyed, but after we did, we added many games to his play repertoire. I will be sharing these modified games later in the chapter.

As speech-language pathologists (SLPs) working with neurodivergent children, we recognize that social skills and play serve as critical developmental foundations. The quality of a child's play experiences directly impacts their communication, language acquisition, and social development. High-quality social skills intervention must foster reciprocity, effective sharing, and social motivation to allow social interaction to become truly enjoyable. This chapter explores evidence-based approaches to enhancing social skills and play within naturalistic contexts, focusing on creating socially interactive teachable moments that support communication development.

Play provides a context for a diverse set of naturally occurring learning opportunities. Research suggests that when we establish an emotional connection during play, more learning takes place. The relationship between play and language development is bidirectional—play supports language acquisition, and language enhances play complexity. For children with communication disorders, particularly for autistic students this relationship becomes even more significant.

Play development follows a relatively predictable sequence, though not necessarily linear. Understanding this sequence helps clinicians identify appropriate intervention points.

Research indicates that autistic children typically engage in less symbolic play, show less variety in their play actions, and demonstrate less complexity in their play scenarios compared to neurotypical peers matched for language age. This highlights the need for targeted play-based interventions that support both play and communication development.

When designing play activities, consider incorporating elements that engage *multiple sensory systems:*

Visually Interesting Activities

- **Balloons:** Use them for shaking, bouncing, playing volleyball, or kicking (with appropriate safety precautions).
- **Wind-up toys:** Create anticipation with "ready, set, go!" routines.
- **Bubbles:** Provide motivation for requesting, commenting, and action words (pop, stomp).

Movement-Based Activities

- **Swings:** Create opportunities for requesting "push," "up," or "all done."
- **Spinning toys:** Incorporate movement that feels good from a sensory standpoint.
- **Therapy balls:** Bounce, roll, or balance together.

Music and Sound Activities

- **Music toys:** Encourage the child to bring the toy to you when it stops.
- **Instruments:** Take turns making sounds.
- **Songs with movements:** Incorporate familiar songs with actions.

Sensory Exploration Activities

- **Sensory bins:** Themed with seasonal items or child's interests.
- **Textured materials:** Incorporate various textures for exploration.
- **Water or sand play:** Provide opportunities for pouring, filling, and emptying.

Research demonstrates that children with autism can develop more sophisticated play skills with structured support. Consider these *evidence-based strategies:*

General Teaching Principles for Play

1. **Follow the child's lead**. Build on their interests and preferred activities.
2. **Model flexible play**. Demonstrate varied ways to interact with the same toy.
3. **Be a giver, not a taker**. Have your own materials rather than taking the child's toys.[1]
4. **Be a partner (not a play director).** We are here to support our students, not dictate what their play should look like.
5. **Use heightened animation and affect**. Be your "level of enthusiastic" to engage interest.
6. **Provide multiple toys**. Have several similar items available for modeling and imitation.
7. **Incorporate pretend play with functional routines**. Model everyday activities like cooking, cleaning, or sleeping.

8. **Alternate preferred and less familiar toys**. Create motivation by balancing highly preferred activities with newer items.
9. **Use visual schedules**. Support play sequences with visual supports when helpful.
10. **Expand play repertoires gradually**. Start with the child's interests and slowly introduce variations.
11. **Offer choices**. Embed choice-making throughout play activities.

Research by Barton et al. (2022)[2] compared the effectiveness of developmental-match versus age-match targets for teaching play skills to autistic children. The study found that children made significantly more progress when intervention focused on developmentally appropriate skills rather than age-matched skills. This finding suggests that SLPs should take these steps:

1. Assess the child's current developmental play level.
2. Target skills that are slightly above their current level (in the zone of proximal development).
3. Use the resource chart above to identify appropriate targets.

MODIFIED LEISURE SKILLS TO INCREASE PLAY AND SOCIAL SKILLS

Games provide natural contexts for practicing turn-taking, following rules, and social communication. However, many games need modification to be accessible for children with social communication challenges. To help my clients I have created a YouTube channel with video examples that you can use in therapy. If a video model is available on my YouTube channel, ABA Speech, it will be noted.

Activity 1: Modified Connect Four (YouTube available)

Connect Four is the first game that I ever modified for a student. I had a student who was very social but who really struggled with task duration and motor planning. I knew that it would be difficult for him to strategize getting four in a row, so I gave it some thought, and modified Connect Four came to life! The goal of the game is not to get four in a row but to *take turns* putting all the pieces in. Here are the steps:

1. Get Connect Four.
2. Ask the student if they want blue or red.
3. Make a pile for the therapist and a pile for the student (Note: Some students may be overwhelmed by having access to all the game pieces so you can give them access to a smaller number of pieces).

4. Demonstrate by taking a turn first.

5. Take turns putting in game pieces.

6. DO NOT require your student to say, "My turn," "Your turn"; this will shape unnatural language.

7. Minimal talking is needed, and the goal is to take balanced turns while engaging in a social interaction.

Activity 2: Modified Simon Says

Modification: It is *always* Simon Says.

1. Tell your student, "We are going to play 'Simon Says.' I am going to do something, and you do it after me."

2. The goal is to engage in a social interaction and to follow directions.

3. Say the direction and do the action. For example, "Simon says touch your ears." (*Touch your ears.*)

4. Other example directions include: Touch your head, touch your belly, touch your nose, put your hands up, clap, stomp your feet, jump, stand up, sit down, shout hooray, twist, make windmill arms.

Activity 3: Modified Musical Chairs

Modification: Do not take away any chairs.

1. Grab as many chairs as you have students.

2. Put the chairs into a circle; you can make this as big or as small as you want.

3. Tell the students, "When I turn the music on, we will walk, and when the music stops you sit down."

4. Show students exactly what you mean by demonstrating an example.

5. Play music that your students love and enjoy. Play the music for a short duration and then stop the music.

Activity 4: Freeze Dancing

1. Tell your students you are going to play "Freeze Dance."

2. Share the directions: "When the music is on, we will dance, and when the music stops, we freeze."

3. Show students exactly what you mean by demonstrating an example.

4. Turn on music your students love. You can also use a brain break video for this by showing a video on YouTube. I love to use "Go Noodle" for this!

5. Play the music for a while and then pause it—FREEZE.

Activity 5: Paper Plate Ice Skating

Paper plate ice skating is one of my favorite activities! I learned about this activity during a music class when my kids were younger. The instructor was very dynamic, and she introduced paper plate ice skating. This activity is affordable—all you need are some paper plates. Put on your favorite song (no ice or snow required), put each foot onto a paper plate, and glide or skate around. When I do this in a group, I am usually the leader—behind me is a student and then an assistant and then a student and then an assistant—you get the idea! It's a fun activity for individual or group sessions!

1. Grab two paper plates per person.
2. Share that "We are going to play paper plate ice skating."
3. Put the paper plates under your shoes.
4. Demonstrate by taking a turn first.
5. Start skating.
6. You can take turns with your student. At first, they are the leader and then you are the leader. Or if you are doing this in a group, follow this pattern if possible: SLP, student, paraprofessional, student, paraprofessional, etc.

Activity 6: Modified Uno (YouTube available)

Modification: Matching Colors

1. Grab the game UNO.
2. Remove the Draw Two, Reverse, Wild, and Skip cards.
3. Put one blue, one red, one yellow, and one green in the center of the table.
4. Explain the rules: "Pick a card and match it to the same color."
5. Demonstrate by taking a turn first.
6. Make a center pile. Take turns picking a card, turning it over, and matching it to the same color card.
7. If it is too difficult for your student to pick from a main pile, a modification based on fine motor needs can be made here.
8. The goal is to take turns until all the cards from the main pile have been matched.

Activity 7: Modified Matching (YouTube available)

Matching for the win! There are a variety of matching games on the market these days, and sometimes they are characters that our students love and enjoy. I set aside 10 matches and place them into a small plastic bag. The first time I play this game with my students I put one part of each match face up. I put the other part of the match face down in one pile. I take turns with the student picking a card—matching to the other card that is identical and face up.

If my student can say what they matched, that is amazing. If my student is not yet speaking, I may narrate the match. "Wow you found another firetruck—awesome matching." As your students learn to play a matching game this way, you can start to systematically turn over the cards that are face up—but don't do this all at once! There is no rush. Enjoy playing this matching game with your students.

1. Grab a matching or memory game.
2. There will be many matches; you will pick 10 complete matches and put these into a plastic baggie.
3. Take one card from each match and put it on the table face up.
4. Take the other cards and put them face down in a pile on the table.
5. Explain the rules: "Pick a card and make a match."
6. Demonstrate by taking a turn first.
7. Take turns picking a card and making a match to a card that is face up.
8. Take turns until all the matches are made.
9. As the student feels more comfortable with the game, you can add more matches and/or start to systematically turn the cards that are face up, face down.

Activity 8: Grocery Store Game (YouTube available)

This is a fun alphabet game!

1. In this game, we take turns thinking of a food or item that we can buy at the grocery store.
2. Write the first letter of half the alphabet on a dry erase board. You can do the entire alphabet, but I find that takes too long, so I break up this game a bit.
3. Explain the rules: "We are going to take turns thinking of a food item or item that we can buy from the grocery store that starts with each letter of the alphabet."
4. Demonstrate by taking a turn first. "A is for apple."
5. Take turns developing words. If you have a dry erase board, you can write the developed words out.
6. Use visuals if your student needs help to develop a word. We have a printable in the supplemental materials that you can use at www.abaspeech.org! It has a visual for each letter of the alphabet.

Activity 9: Modified Button Art

1. Button art is a fun material that I have been using with my students for over 10 years.
2. It comes with a variety of pictures and colored buttons.
3. Tell your student, "We are going to make a button art picture."

4. Give them a choice of designs that can be made. "Do you want to make a dinosaur or house?"
5. Put the design on.
6. Sort out the buttons that are needed to make the picture.
7. Explain the rules: "We are going to make a design. We will take turns picking a button and matching it."
8. Demonstrate by taking a turn first. Pick a button and match it to the correct color on the button art design.
9. Take turns picking a button and matching it on the design.
10. After all the buttons are used and the design is made, encourage your student to label the design "I made a dinosaur," "dinosaur."

Activity 10: Would You Rather Dessert (YouTube available)

1. "Would you rather" questions are a great way to work on social language skills.
2. Explain the rules: "We are going to play *Would You Rather.*"
3. Go to the URL for the "Would You Rather Dessert" on the ABA Speech YouTube channel.
4. Press play.
5. There are 15 examples. Each example has two choices, and it allows you about 15 seconds to make a choice.
6. Demonstrate by taking your turn first. Sometimes I take turns with this activity, or we both answer the same question.

Parents are children's first and most important play partners. Effective parent coaching can significantly enhance generalization of play skills to home and community settings:

Parent Coaching Strategies

1. **Identify existing routines**. Build on activities already occurring in the home.
2. **Model and explain**. Demonstrate play facilitation techniques with clear explanations.
3. **Practice with feedback**. Provide opportunities for parents to practice with supportive feedback.
4. **Focus on enjoyment**. Emphasize the relationship and enjoyment rather than perfect implementation.
5. **Build gradually**. Start with brief, successful interactions before extending duration.
6. **Provide visual supports**. Create simple handouts or videos for reference.
7. **Celebrate successes**. Acknowledge and reinforce parents' successful implementation.

As we integrate research findings into clinical practice, several key principles emerge for SLPs:

1. **Prioritize developmental appropriateness**. Target skills based on the child's developmental level rather than chronological age.
2. **Balance structure and naturalistic approaches**. Combine the benefits of structured teaching with naturalistic contexts.
3. **Focus on engagement and motivation**. Make social interaction intrinsically rewarding.
4. **Consider sensory needs**. Incorporate sensory elements that support regulation and engagement.
5. **Use multidisciplinary perspectives**. Draw from developmental, behavioral, and sensory processing frameworks.
6. **Document functional outcomes**. Measure success by the child's ability to participate in meaningful social interactions.

SUMMARY

Play serves as a critical context for developing communication, language, and social skills. By implementing evidence-based strategies that focus on engagement, developmental appropriateness, and naturalistic interactions, SLPs can significantly enhance outcomes for children with social communication challenges. The integration of sensory social routines, structured play interventions, and game adaptations within a collaborative framework provides a comprehensive approach to addressing the complex relationship between play and communication development.

NOTES

1. Tamara Kasper CCC-SLP, BCBA, personal communication.
2. Barton, E. E., Pokorski, E. A., Sweeney, E. M., Velez, M., Gossett, S., Qiu, J., Flaherty, C., & Domingo, M. (2018). An empirical examination of effective practices for teaching board game play to young children. *Journal of Positive Behavior Interventions*, *20*(3), 138–148. https://doi.org/10.1177/1098300717753833.

CHAPTER 5

Beyond Single Words: Teaching Expressive Language Students Will Use

Several years ago, I was the lead speech therapist at an amazing program for autistic learners. We had four classrooms for students ranging from preschool to high school. I loved how specific and collaborative the educational model was at this program.

I remember working with a student who was in the preschool classroom. He was four years old and had an autism diagnosis. He was not yet speaking and seemed to enjoy our therapy sessions. He was using a static augmentative and alternative communication (AAC) device. So, the buttons were preprogrammed for him. He used his device but not consistently. When I met him, he did not have any verbal imitation or expressive language goals.

I was out at recess one day at the top of the slide and I remember turning around to hear this student, who had never spoken, yelling at another student! He was saying, "Hey it's my turn!" He really wanted to go down the slide next. My jaw dropped! I had been working with him for about a month and had not heard him verbalize. This was an amazing moment!

We went on to harness that verbal communication, not only at recess but across his entire day. He continued to have access to the AAC device as a backup, but he became a fully verbal communicator.

This chapter offers a framework for systematically helping your students increase their expressive language skills. We will focus on first words and how to expand their vocabulary. In addition, we will cover some strategies for verbal expression and clarity of speech toward the end of the chapter. The goal is to help you feel more confident with expressive language.

As Dr. Mark Sundberg wisely points out, our focus needs to shift toward helping students use the vocabulary they already have in various ways and contexts. We want to move them toward less restrictive, more natural settings while emphasizing social interactions, independence, emotional regulation, and problem-solving skills.

This chapter takes you on a journey through a comprehensive, developmentally informed approach to strengthening expressive language skills. We're not just talking about getting kids to say more words; we're talking about helping learners become independent, confident communicators who can navigate successfully across all the environments in their lives.

THE IMPORTANCE OF REQUESTING

Requesting is foundational to everything else we do. Research tells us that "requests are first in the language repertoire learned by all children and are very important for the early development of language and for day-to-day verbal interaction of children and adults."[1] But here's what makes this so beautiful in practice.

When children truly understand that their communication has power—that asking for a movie results in watching that movie, or requesting a walk leads to taking that walk—something magical happens. They develop what we call "learner history." It's like a light bulb moment where they realize, "Hey, when I communicate, good things happen!" This becomes the foundation for every future communication attempt.

The key is starting with specific requests rather than general words like "please." If a child absolutely loves Legos, we work on requesting "Lego." If a child is attached to a particular teddy bear, we start with requesting "bear." This specificity matters because it connects directly to what motivates the child. Then we embed these opportunities throughout the entire day, which really requires true teamwork between families, therapists, and educators.

What's wonderful is that every child's communication mode can be different. Some will use verbal approximations—saying "app" for "apple" is perfectly acceptable and something we can build on. Others might use pictures, sign language, or AAC devices. The important thing is that every single student has a way to communicate spontaneously with their world.

What would this look like in therapy? We want to make sure that we work on requesting in a way that empowers our students and helps them feel confident in their communication. We will spend time talking about examples of how to work on this but first a big DON'T to keep in mind. Don't have a student request food items. Food is a basic need, and we should not work on requesting it! This means we should not have a student request every goldfish they have at snack. We should not have a student request each pretzel they have when they get home from school. And if you see others doing it—kindly let them know that there are better, more ethical ways to work on requesting.

Requesting Examples

1. The speech therapist is blowing bubbles. The student pops the bubbles and requests "bubbles" to have the therapist blow more.
2. The speech therapist is pushing the child on a swing. They love this! The momentum stops and they want another push, the student requests "push."
3. The student is playing Connect Four and is given a choice between the red or yellow tokens. The student requests "yellow."
4. The student and therapist are playing with a farm toy. The student has the cow and horse. The therapist has the pig and goat. The student requests "pig" "goat."
5. The student is playing on a mini trampoline but is a little fearful of jumping alone, so the therapist takes their hands to help them. The student requests "jump."
6. The student is frustrated because they can't open their juice box straw at lunch. The therapist works on requesting "help."
7. The student is participating in a field day activity, it is loud and overwhelming. The student requests "all done."
8. The class is listening to a song from a new movie the student loves. When the song is over, the student wants to hear another song. The student requests "music."
9. The student has a choice of centers, and he requests "book" for the book center.
10. The student is doing a brain break with the class. She loves this and requests "dance" to see her teacher dance too.

WHEN FIRST WORDS ARE SPOKEN

According to the American Speech-Language-Hearing Association (ASHA), most typically developing children say their first word around 12 months of age.[2]

- By 12 months:
  - Children usually say one or two words (like "mama," "dada," or "ball") that are used intentionally and consistently.
  - These words usually refer to familiar people or objects and are spoken with meaning.

It is important to note that about 25–30% of autistic children will never acquire complex speech.[3] So, it is important that we help all our students find a way to communicate with the world. For some students this will be through verbal communication and for other students this will be through sign, pictures, AAC, or a combination of these forms of communication.

Okay, now we are ready for some single words!

First Words

I always tell parents and therapists a student's first word is not going to be labeling a flashcard! First words are usually heard through functional and fun routines. We may hear that first word through some of our joint attention activities that we have already been using in therapy. Here are some general strategies and activities that may set the stage for those first words:

1. **Keep things fun and functional.** We need to connect socially with our students. Research shows that when we have an emotional connection with our students, their learning will increase!
2. **Don't demand communication.** Lessen the demand. We need to focus on praising all verbal communicative attempts. These would include gestures, babbling, and other noises.
3. **Don't bombard the student with questions.** This puts students on the spot and is not the best way to spend our time in therapy. It may feel funny at first, but we want to talk and *pause*. That pause is where the magic happens!
4. **Teach functional words.** Teach words that are motivating and important for your student. Don't just pick words from a curriculum or a set of lists that are not meaningful.
5. **Use more specific words.** Don't teach words like *more* or *please* as first words. Vague words are not as powerful for our students. If they love music, teach the word *music*. If they love bubbles, teach the word *bubbles*.

The Three-term Contingency in Real Life

Every teaching opportunity can be understood through the A-B-C framework: **antecedent**, **behavior**, and **consequence**. But in naturalistic settings, this doesn't feel clinical or artificial. Picture a favorite toy placed just out of reach—that's our antecedent. The child points and says "baby"—that's our behavior. We respond with "That is a baby" and give them the toy— that's our consequence, which naturally reinforces the communication attempt.

These opportunities happen constantly throughout the day once you start noticing them. A puzzle with a missing piece creates a natural need to communicate. Putting art supplies out with crayons just out of reach sets up a perfect requesting opportunity. The key is being a "giver, not a taker"—we arrange environments thoughtfully rather than taking things away from children.[4]

The Art of Modeling and Narrating

Consistent exposure to developmentally appropriate language models significantly enhances language skills. This is where we become natural narrators of our world. If I'm working with blocks and modeling single words, I might say, "Block." If I'm targeting phrases, I'll say, "Big block." For longer utterances, I might say, "Stack the block."

The magic happens in what we call *recasting*—repeating what the child attempted but expanding on it. If a child says "bubba," I might respond with "Yeah, bubbles! Woo, I can't get enough of bubbles!" The child gets exposed to longer phrases and grammatical structures without being required to repeat them. This takes the pressure off while still providing rich language input.

I always tell parents and staff not to bombard students with questions. I try to remind parents and team members that if we ask too many questions, like "What is that? What does it say? What color? What do you do with it?" in rapid succession, we may turn a new communicator off to communication! Be careful here.

EXPRESSIVE LANGUAGE DEVELOPMENT

Labeling

Please work on labeling preferred words! We don't, I repeat, we don't start working on non-preferred labeling targets. Labeling might be very difficult for your student. Remember, we are here to support and make therapy fun and functional (Figure 5.1).

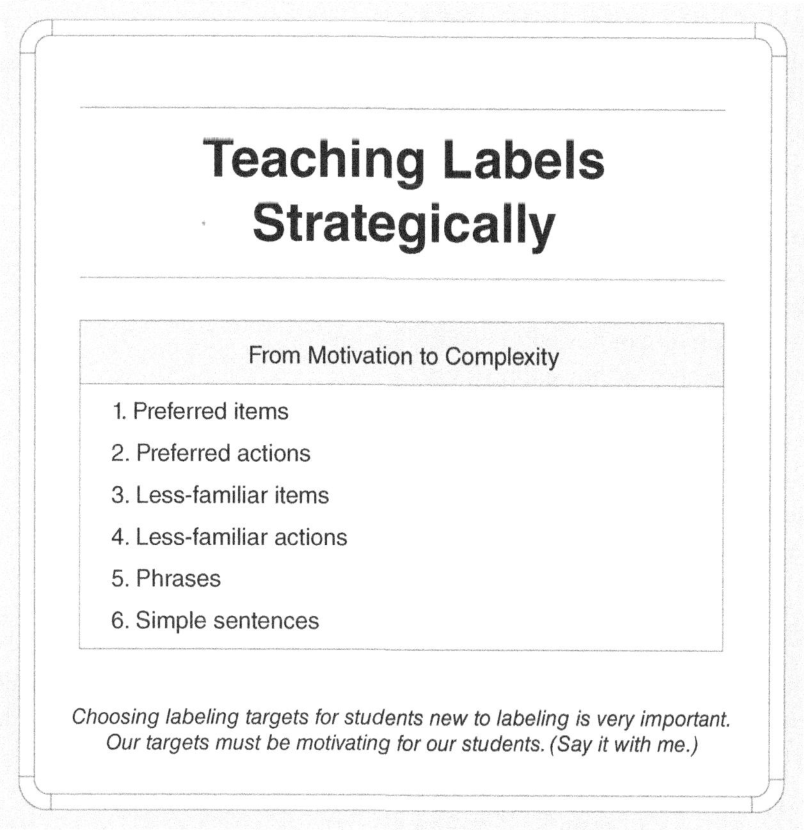

FIGURE 5.1   Teaching labels strategically: from motivation to complexity.

1. Preferred items
2. Preferred actions
3. Less-familiar items
4. Less-familiar actions
5. Phrases
6. Simple sentences

When our students are beginning to say their first words, we can start to work on labeling. Labeling is a very important skill and helps our students increase their overall expressive language. We can work on this skill through naturalistic contexts, structured contexts, or a bit of both! What is most important are the words that we choose to teach.

Therapy Tips

Labeling Preferred Actions

A student, Maverick, is working on labeling actions using the present progressive form of the action. Labeling actions is a new skill and very difficult for him. Due to these two factors, the team has decided to work on actions that are very motivating and preferred. The current target is "eating." The team has prepared three pictures of eating. One is a boy eating pizza, one is a girl eating broccoli, and one is a woman eating fries. Three cards are chosen to embed work on generalization of the skill of labeling. Planning ahead for generalization will help him label a variety of pictures of actions he works on at school.

Therapy Snapshot
 SLP: Presents picture of boy eating pizza
 Maverick: (No answer)
 SLP: Presents picture of boy eating pizza, "Eating."
 SLP: Presents picture of boy eating pizza
 Maverick: "eating"
 SLP: "Great work, he is eating!"
 SLP: Presents picture of boy eating pizza
 Maverick: "eating"
 SLP: "Wow, great work Maverick! The boy is eating."

Labeling Preferred Nouns

Maverick is working on labeling preferred nouns. Labeling nouns is a new and emerging skill and is currently very difficult for him. Due to these two factors, the team has decided to target highly preferred and motivating items. The current target is "car." The team has prepared three pictures of different types of cars. One is a blue sports car, one is a red family car, and one is a picture of his own family car. These cards are used to support generalization of the skill across different pictures. Planning ahead for generalization will help Maverick label a variety of pictures of familiar, motivating items.

Therapy Snapshot

SLP: Presents picture of the blue car.
Maverick: (No answer)
SLP: Presents same picture again. Points to the picture.
Maverick: "Car."
SLP: "Nice job! That is a car!"
SLP: Presents picture of the same blue car.
Maverick: "Car."
SLP: "Great work, Maverick! It is a car."

Labeling Less-familiar Actions

Maverick has been making great progress with labeling familiar actions; the team has decided to introduce labeling less-familiar actions. This will help Maverick broaden his overall vocabulary development. The current target is "brushing." The team has prepared three pictures of brushing. One is a boy brushing teeth, one is a girl brushing hair, and the other is a boy brushing a horse's hair. Three cards are chosen to embed work on generalization of the skill of labeling. His class at school visits a local farm to interact with the animals once a month so this is a helpful target!

Therapy Snapshot

SLP: Presents picture of boy brushing teeth
Maverick: "Brushing"
SLP: "That is right—amazing work!"
SLP: Presents picture of girl brushing hair
Maverick: "Brushing"
SLP: "Great work, she is brushing!"

Labeling Less-familiar Nouns

Maverick is making a lot of progress with labeling familiar nouns; the team would like to start incorporating work on less familiar nouns. These targets have been chosen as they are a part of Maverick's environment. Maverick has a dog named Poppy. So, ***dog*** is the current noun target. The team has prepared three pictures of dogs. One is a small cream-colored dog. One is a picture of the same breed as Poppy but a different color, and one is a big black dog. Three cards are chosen to embed work on generalization of the skill of labeling.

Therapy Snapshot

　　SLP: Presents picture of the small cream-colored dog.

　　Maverick: "dog"

　　SLP: "That is a dog!"

　　SLP: Presents picture of the same breed as Poppy.

　　Maverick: "dog"

　　SLP: "You got it!"

　　SLP: Presents a picture of the big black dog.

　　Maverick: "dog"

　　SLP: "Wow, amazing work Maverick, those are all dogs!"

MOVING BEYOND SINGLE WORDS

Once learners have mastered basic requesting and imitation, we can focus on using vocabulary in varied contexts and developing more sophisticated language structures. The developmental progression looks like around 12–22 months, we see agent-action and action-object combinations like "eating pizza." By 22–26 months, children typically put together subject-verb-object constructions like "The boy is eating pizza."

I love working on phrase and sentence construction because you can see the progression happen in real time. I might hold up a picture and ask, "What is he doing?" and the student responds with "washing hair." Then I'll show multiple examples—different people, different contexts—because we want to teach loosely and plan for generalization from the very beginning.

The goal isn't to be rigid in our instruction. In natural conversation, people don't always say things the same way, so I vary my questions. Sometimes I'll ask, "What's happening?" or "Can you tell me a sentence about this one?" This flexibility helps students learn that language is adaptable and functional across different situations.

Beyond Single Words Examples

When my students can label a variety of nouns and actions, I like to start working on phrase construction using the mastered nouns and actions (see Figure 5.2). For example, these are good starting nouns and actions:

Nouns

    a. Bubble

    b. Pizza

    c. Apple

    d. Hair

   e. Teeth

   f. Basketball

   g. Mommy

   h. Daddy

   i. Water

   j. Juice

Actions

   a. Blowing

   b. Eating

   c. Brushing

   d. Playing

   e. Hugging

   f. Drinking

When working on phrase construction, I would work on the following examples. These examples would allow us to utilize labels that are already in the students labeling repertoire.

FIGURE 5.2 Action builder cards.

Phrase Construction

a. Blowing bubbles
b. Eating pizza
c. Eating apple
d. Brushing hair
e. Brushing teeth
f. Playing basketball
g. Hugging mommy
h. Hugging daddy
i. Drinking water
j. Drinking juice

Once my student has many phrases in their vocabulary, I will start to work on sentence construction. This will be very individualized for your students. You might work on simple sentences first or phrases and sentences together. Making an individualized plan for each student is helpful.

Sentence Construction

a. She is blowing bubbles.
b. He is eating pizza.
c. She is eating an apple.
d. He is brushing his hair.
e. She is brushing her teeth.
f. They are playing basketball.
g. He is hugging mommy.
h. She is hugging daddy.
i. They are drinking water.
j. They are drinking juice.

These examples come from The Action Builder Cards. I created the action builder cards in 2017 to help my students increase their communication skills. There are 100 cards with 13 frequently occurring actions represented. These cards are now available in a digital format.

Understanding Grammatical Development

When we're working on grammatical markers, it's incredibly helpful to understand typical acquisition patterns. Present progressive "-ing" typically develops between 19 and 28 months, regular plural "-s" between 27 and 33 months, and regular past-tense "-ed" between 26 and

48 months. This information helps us set appropriate expectations and choose meaningful targets.

I like to use visual supports that combine pictures with text, focusing on scenarios from the child's actual daily life. Instead of abstract examples, we might work on "Yesterday we walked to the park" when we did walk to the park the day before. This connection to real experience makes the learning stick.

Irregular past-tense verbs present a unique challenge because they're few in number but high in frequency. Words like *went, ate,* and *gave* come up constantly in children's conversations. I remember kids coming back from spring break wanting to tell me about their trips, and they'd focus on food: "I had pancakes in the morning and then we had ice cream at night." Teaching these irregular forms helps children tell their stories more completely.

Moving beyond simple labeling to robust vocabulary understanding involves teaching students to engage with words in multiple ways. When a student can label something as a "bike," that's wonderful, but can they tell me three things about a bike? Can they explain what you do with it, what category it belongs to, or use it in a sentence?

I love using current events materials like "News to You" because it provides curricular vocabulary that students encounter in their classrooms. When I worked as a school-based therapist, I'd collaborate with classroom teachers who would use this resource on the smart board. Students who could read would read the words they knew, and if they had trouble with a word, they could tap the board, and it would say the word for them.

This approach creates shared goals between speech therapy and classroom instruction. If we're reading about national trails and the student is working on the word "bike," we can explore that word thoroughly. I might ask open-ended questions like "Tell me a couple things about a bike" or provide scaffolded support with specific questions about features, functions, and categories.

VERBAL COMMUNICATION

Assessment like we discussed in Chapter 1 is important. We want to know what sounds are in the student's inventory. This will help us develop a plan on what sounds and/or syllable shapes to focus on first in therapy. It's important to take an inventory of what words and sounds we have heard our student say. This information, along with developmental norms and our student's motivation and interest, will allow us to develop functional verbal targets. It is very important that we are working on verbal imitation targets that are meaningful for our students.

Once we have our assessment in place, pick three to five meaningful verbal imitation targets for our student. Work on these targets in a way that is fun, functional, and naturalistic. Once a target is mastered or has met criterion, share with the rest of the team so that this verbal imitation target can be generalized across the student's day.

Activity Ideas

These are five words from my verbal imitation guide and play-based ways to work on these verbal imitation targets:

1. *Mama*
   Activity: Baby Dolls
   Have one to three baby dolls. Tell the student "Baby is hungry, she needs a bottle from her mama." Encourage the student to say *mama* after your model.

2. *Baa Baa*
   Activity: Singing "Old MacDonald"
   Use a sheep toy or a laminated sheep picture. Sing "Old MacDonald Had a Farm." Encourage your student to say *baa baa* after your verbal model.

3. *Up*
   Activity: Bubbles
   Blow bubbles toward the ceiling (Figure 5.3). As the bubbles climb higher, model the word *up*.

FIGURE 5.3 Blowing bubbles models the word up.

4. *Go*

Activity: Car Ramp

Use cars on a ramp or a track. Hold the car and say, "Ready ... set ... go!" Then pause to let the child say *go!*

---

5. *Eat*

Activity: Feed the Stuffed Animals

Use toy food and stuffed animals. Say, "Let's feed the bear! Eat, eat, eat!"

Model: "Eat!" as you give food to the toy and let your client say *eat* after you.

Our goal is to work on verbal imitation and, as our student makes progress, to encourage spontaneous use of these words in the natural environment.

The Power of Collaboration

Successful expressive language development absolutely requires coordination among speech-language pathologists, board certified behavior analysts, special education teachers, families, and paraprofessionals. Each team member brings unique expertise and perspectives that benefit the child.

When I worked in schools, some of my most successful cases involved close collaboration with classroom teachers. We'd share goals, coordinate materials, and ensure that what we worked on in speech therapy connected meaningfully to what happened in the classroom. This shared approach prevented skill isolation and promoted genuine generalization.

Planning for Generalization from Day One

From the very beginning of intervention, we need to plan for skill transfer across settings, people, and contexts. Multiple example training means teaching various examples of the same concept. If we're working on requesting, we don't just practice with one toy—we practice with multiple preferred items across different activities.

Loose training involves varying our instructions, materials, and contexts deliberately. Natural environment instruction takes place in real-world settings where children will need to use their skills. Maintenance programming ensures that mastered skills continue to be practiced and refined over time.

Every learner's communication journey is beautifully unique. Some children will use verbal approximations that we can gradually shape toward clearer speech. Others will rely on visual supports like pictures, symbols, or written words. Some will utilize sign language either with or without voice, while others will access AAC devices for complex communication needs.

The key is not forcing every child into the same mold but rather finding the communication mode that works best for each individual. Goals must align with chronological age expectations while considering developmental prerequisites, individual strengths and interests, and functional relevance to the child's daily life.

I've learned that pushing too hard or too fast can slow progress. Goals need to be ambitious enough to promote growth while remaining achievable given the child's current skill level. When I see students struggling with targets or becoming frustrated in sessions, I often step back and ask whether we have the necessary foundation skills in place.

Sometimes this means spending more time on prerequisites such as joint attention or imitation before moving to more advanced expressive language targets. Other times, it means adjusting our approach or finding more motivating materials. The child's response guides our decision-making more than any predetermined curriculum.

What Sessions Actually Look Like

A comprehensive 30- to 45-minute session might flow naturally from greeting and choice-making into structured practice with visual supports, then natural application during preferred activities, followed by literacy integration with book reading, and ending with review and preview. But this structure remains flexible based on the child's needs and interests on any given day.

The materials we choose make a huge difference. High-interest activities that match the child's preferences and developmental level create natural motivation. Visual supports provide scaffolding when needed. A good literature collection offers countless opportunities for interaction and engagement. Sensory materials naturally promote communication, and technology tools can expand possibilities for complex expression.

Sometimes progress stalls despite our best efforts. When data indicates limited growth, we need to reassess prerequisites, modify our approach, adjust targets, increase support, or seek consultation from specialists. The key is remaining flexible and responsive rather than rigidly sticking to plans that aren't working.

Communication difficulties often coincide with challenging behaviors, which makes perfect sense when you think about it. If I couldn't effectively communicate my needs, I'd probably get frustrated too! Teaching replacement behaviors gives students appropriate ways to communicate their needs. We address the underlying functions that challenging behavior serves while modifying environments to reduce frustration and increase success.

CONCLUSION

Strengthening expressive language skills in autistic learners requires a comprehensive, individualized, and naturalistic approach that truly honors each child's unique communication journey. By building on solid foundations of requesting and imitation, incorporating developmentally appropriate targets, and maintaining focus on functional, socially significant outcomes, we help learners develop the expressive language skills they need to navigate their world successfully.

Remember, communication isn't just about producing words—it's about connecting with others, expressing thoughts and needs, and participating meaningfully in the social world. When we approach expressive language intervention with this broader perspective, embedding systematic instruction within natural, engaging contexts, we create the conditions for authentic, lasting communication growth.

Success in expressive language development ultimately depends on our ability to be responsive to each learner's needs, flexible in our approaches, and persistent in our commitment to helping every child find their voice and use it confidently across all areas of their life. Every child has something important to say. Our job is to help them find the best way to say it.

NOTES

1. Sundberg, M. L. (2008). *The Verbal Behavior Milestones Assessment and Placement Program: The VB-MAPP.* Concord, CA: AVB Press.

2. American Speech-Language-Hearing Association. Communication Milestones. American Speech-Language-Hearing Association.

3. Tager-Flusberg, H., & Kasari, C. (2013). Minimally verbal school-aged children with autism spectrum disorder: the neglected end of the spectrum. *Autism Research* (official journal of the International Society for Autism Research), *6*(6), 468–478.

4. I first heard this phrase used by my friend Tamara Kasper in a training she did in 2010.

CHAPTER 6

Teaching Receptive Language That Sticks: Moving Beyond Rote Responses

I was always excited to work with Noah; he was a preschool-aged student who loved center time, music therapy, and talking to his peers. He had therapy once a week individually and once a week in a group. When I went to probe his receptive language skills, I was really surprised that he was not able to answer simple *wh-* questions like "What is your name?" "When is your birthday?" "What is your favorite snack?" I thought with his ability to talk freely that he would be able to answer these questions. This made me realize early on that direct assessment and systematic instruction of receptive language skills was essential!

Based on Noah's difficulty with comprehension skills, we developed a plan that started with filling in the blanks and progressed through answering personal safety questions, *wh-* questions with a visual through social language questions. With a bit of direct instruction, Noah's receptive language skills flourished. In this chapter we will discuss ways to support your student's receptive language skills too.

When parents bring their child to see you for the first time, parents are usually concerned primarily with getting their child to talk. It's natural for families to focus on expressive language—after all, speaking is the most visible form of communication. But as speech-language pathologists working with autistic learners, we know there's often a more fundamental challenge underneath: receptive language difficulties.

Picture this scenario: You're working with Marcus, a four-year-old autistic student. His parents proudly tell you he can recite entire scenes from his favorite movie and knows all the dinosaur names. Yet when you ask him, "What did you do at school today?" or "Do you have a headache?" he doesn't respond consistently. This disconnect between what appears to be advanced language knowledge and actual comprehension is a hallmark of autism that we must address systematically.

RECEPTIVE LANGUAGE

Understanding language—what we call **receptive language** or **language comprehension**—forms the foundation for all other communication skills. Without this solid base, expressive language remains fragmented, social communication suffers, and academic learning becomes increasingly challenging. This chapter will equip you with evidence-based strategies to assess and strengthen the receptive language skills of your autistic students, setting them up for meaningful communication success.

Receptive language encompasses everything a child understands about language, from recognizing their name to following complex, multistep directions. It includes understanding vocabulary, grammar, question forms, and the ability to process and integrate linguistic information in real time.

Autistic learners often present with a unique receptive language profile that differs significantly from both typically developing children and those with other developmental delays. Understanding these differences is crucial for effective intervention planning.

One of the most striking patterns we see in autism is when expressive language appears to exceed receptive language abilities. Maria, age five, might be able to recite complex phrases from her favorite books or repeat sophisticated vocabulary, yet struggle to understand simple directions like "Get your shoes."

This pattern occurs because much of the "expressive language" we're hearing may actually be **echolalia**—the repetition of words, phrases, or entire segments without full comprehension of meaning. While echolalia serves important developmental functions and shouldn't be discouraged, we must be careful not to overestimate a child's true language comprehension based on their verbal output.

Many autistic students demonstrate what we might call "part versus whole" processing differences. They may understand individual vocabulary words but struggle when those words are combined into longer, more complex utterances. For instance, a child might recognize "shoes," "door," and "by" as separate concepts but cannot process the integrated meaning of "Get your shoes—they're by the door."

This processing difference means we must be strategic about how we present language to our students, often breaking down complex directions into smaller, more manageable chunks while gradually building toward more sophisticated language comprehension.

Rather than processing language word by word, many autistic learners are "chunk learners." They may acquire entire phrases as single units. A child might say, "Where'd it go?" perfectly but not demonstrate understanding of individual question words, pronouns, or verb tenses within that phrase. This learning style has implications for how we teach receptive language. We need to ensure that students truly understand component parts, not just memorized wholes.

Autistic students often show remarkable comprehension within their areas of intense interest while struggling with more general language concepts. A child fascinated by trains might understand complex vocabulary related to locomotives, tracks, and schedules but struggle with basic body parts or common household items. While we should celebrate and utilize these strengths, we must ensure comprehension skills generalize beyond special interests.

The social challenges inherent in autism directly impact receptive language development. Language learning typically occurs through social interaction: Children tune into caregivers, attend to their communication attempts, and gradually link meaning with words through shared experiences. When social engagement is challenging, this natural language learning process is disrupted.

Students who struggle with joint attention, social motivation, or sensory processing may miss countless opportunities to connect meaning with words. They might not naturally orient to their communication partner's voice, follow pointing gestures, or engage in the back-and-forth interactions that build language comprehension.

ASSESSMENT CONSIDERATIONS

While standardized assessments provide valuable information, they often fail to capture the full picture of an autistic student's receptive language abilities. Many autistic learners perform inconsistently in formal testing situations due to factors like sensory sensitivities, anxiety, or difficulty with the testing format itself.

One assessment that is more from the BCBA part of my world is called The Verbal Behavior Milestones and Assessment and Placement Program (VB-MAPP). I discuss this program briefly in Chapter 1. When I started using this assessment over 15 years ago, it changed the way that I assessed and provided intervention for students who needed support in receptive language skills. Often, it was difficult to assess my students' receptive language skills, but the VB-MAPP gave me much needed guidance that I have used and incorporated into my assessments and interventions. Let's look at some of the areas that we can address in assessment and if needed, in intervention:

1. Receptive identification of an *item* or *pictured item* in an array of at least three cards
2. Receptive identification of an *action* in an array of at least three cards
3. Receptive identification of an *item* in a book
4. Receptive identification of an *action* in a book
5. Receptive identification of an item based on its *function*
6. Receptive identification of an item based on its *features*

7. Filling in the blank for common phrases
8. Answering personal safety questions
9. Answering *wh-* questions within a book *with* a visual present
10. Answering *social language* questions *with* a visual present
11. Answering *wh-* questions within a book *without* a visual present
12. Answering *social language* questions *without* a visual present

I will discuss these examples in more detail regarding how to support learners in strengthening these overall comprehension skills.

RECEPTIVE LANGUAGE DEVELOPMENT

One of the most powerful approaches for building receptive language with autistic learners involves presenting multiple examples of the same concept across various contexts. Rather than teaching vocabulary or concepts in isolation, systematically vary the examples while keeping the target constant.

If you're working on understanding "big" and "little," don't just use the same two balls session after session. Include big and little cars, blocks, cups, books, and people in pictures. This helps students extract the essential features of size concepts rather than forming narrow, context-specific associations.

The research strongly supports this approach. Studies consistently show that students who receive multiple exemplar training demonstrate better generalization of learned skills compared to those who practice with limited examples.

Many autistic learners are strong visual processors, and we can leverage this strength to support receptive language development. However, visual supports should enhance, not replace, auditory language input.

Consider using:

- Picture cards or symbols paired with verbal directions
- Visual schedules showing steps of complex tasks
- Written words alongside spoken instructions for readers
- Gestures and pointing to highlight key information
- Environmental arrangement to reduce distractions and highlight important materials

The goal is gradual fading of visual supports as auditory comprehension improves, but don't rush this process. Some students may always benefit from visual enhancement of verbal information.

Develop a consistent prompting hierarchy that you use across activities. This might include:

1. **Clear verbal instruction** (appropriately paced and simplified)
2. **Verbal instruction with gesture** (pointing, demonstrating)

Always start with the least support necessary and provide additional help only when needed. This ensures that students don't become overly dependent on prompts while still receiving necessary support for success.

While structured activities have their place, comprehension skills must ultimately generalize to natural environments. Look for opportunities to embed receptive language targets into functional, meaningful activities.

During snack time, work on following directions about food distribution. During cleanup, practice spatial concepts and sequencing. During play activities, target action words and descriptive language. This naturalistic approach helps students understand that language comprehension has real-world relevance and application.

Therapy Tips

Receptive identification of an item or pictured item in an array of at least three cards
Work on items that are preferred at first and then work on functional items too. A student, Shay, is working on identifying preferred items in a field of three cards.
SLP: Puts out three flashcards on the table: "Where is the car?"
Shay: Points to the car
SLP: "That is a car, great job!"

Receptive identification of an action in an array of at least three cards
SLP: Puts out three flashcards on the table: "Who is eating?"
Shay: Does not respond
SLP: "Who is eating?" Holds up the picture of eating
SLP: Puts out three different flashcards: "Who is eating?"
Shay: Points to the student who is eating
SLP: "Yes eating! Wow, great job!"

Receptive identification of an item in a book
SLP: Is reading *Goodnight Gorilla*. On the page with the giraffe, asks, "Where is the giraffe?"
Shay: Points to the giraffe
SLP: "Hello, Giraffe."

Receptive identification of an item based on its function
SLP: Puts out three mini objects on the carpet: "Which one do you wear?"
Shay: Grabs the hat
SLP: "We wear a hat!"

Filling in the blank for common phrases

   SLP: Gets out bubbles, takes the bubble wand out and says, "Ready, set, _______"
   Shay: Says, "go!"
   SLP: Blows bubbles

Answering personal safety questions

   SLP: What is your name?
   Shay: No response
   SLP: "What is your name?" Presents visual of the student's name.
   Shay: "Shay"
   SLP: "What is your name?"
   Shay: "Shay"
   SLP: "Wow, amazing, Shay!"

Answering *wh-* questions within a book with a visual present

   SLP: Presents the book *Pete the Cat and the Perfect Pizza Party*. Shows a page and says, "They have pretzels." "What do they have?"
   Shay: Activates the pretzels icon on their AAC device.
   SLP: "Yes, pretzels."

This can also be accomplished by using adapted books. I made many adapted books for my clients. Each adapted book is about a themed event: the farm, the weather, etc. Each page has one picture and one sentence (Figure 6.1). This allows the clinician to read the page and, when applicable, ask the student a question. The student can use the picture as

FIGURE 6.1   Page from an adaptive book.

a visual to help support their understanding of language. This is a wonderful first step on the road to strengthening overall comprehension skills. Make sure to check for the books I am sharing with our readers: *Our Trip to the Farm* and *All About the Weather*. These can be used by printing them out or sharing them on an iPad or smartboard.

Answering social language questions with a visual present

SLP: Presents the "Let's Talk Boom Card" and asks, "What would you want to eat for breakfast?"

Student: Looks at the pictures, points to the pancakes, and says, "Pancakes are yummy."

In general, as students master simpler discriminations, gradually increase complexity:

- Add more choices (field of three, four, eventually unlimited).
- Include similar items (cookie versus cracker versus cake).
- Use less preferred items.
- Introduce more abstract concepts.
- Work across different materials (real objects, photographs, line drawings, written words).

Direction Following Progressions

Understanding spatial relationships is crucial for following directions and academic success. Follow typical developmental progressions:

- **24 months:** in, on
- **36 months:** under
- **40 months:** next to
- **48 months:** behind, in front of
- **60+ months:** before, after, between

Systematically build your student's ability to follow increasingly complex directions:

Single-step directions:

- "Come here."
- "Get the ball."
- "Put on your hat."

Two-step directions:

- "Get the marker and give it to your teacher."
- "Throw this away and then line up at the door."

Multistep directions:

- "First hang up your backpack, then wash your hands, and finally sit at the table."

Conditional directions:

- "If you hear your name, stand up."
- "When I ring the bell, put your materials away."

Use real, functional directions whenever possible rather than artificial commands. This helps students understand the practical value of following directions and increases motivation for compliance.

Preposition and Spatial Concept Development

Use real objects and encourage students to manipulate materials rather than simply pointing to pictures. "Put the ball in the box" is more meaningful when students perform the action with three-dimensional objects.

Create obstacle courses or movement activities that incorporate spatial concepts: "Crawl under the table, then jump on the mat, and finally hide behind the chair." This combination of language and movement can be particularly effective for students who learn best through kinesthetic experiences.

Some autistic learners have minimal or no spoken language, which can make assessing receptive language particularly challenging. These students may understand much more than they can demonstrate through traditional means.

Alternative Response Modes

Teach and accept various ways students can show understanding:

- Pointing to pictures or objects
- Following through with requested actions
- Using simple gestures or signs
- Activating voice output devices
- Eye gazing or other subtle movements

Augmentative and alternative communication (AAC) systems can both support and reveal receptive language abilities. A student might not be able to say *bathroom* but can point to a bathroom symbol when you ask, "Where do we go to wash our hands?"

Use AAC systems during receptive language activities to provide multiple ways for students to demonstrate understanding without the pressure of verbal expression.

Many autistic students struggle with directions that contain multiple pieces of information, even when they understand each component individually. This challenge requires systematic intervention.

Collaborating with Educational Teams

Work closely with teachers to ensure receptive language goals are addressed throughout the school day. Provide specific strategies in which staff can:

- Simplify complex directions by breaking them into smaller steps.
- Use visual supports to enhance verbal instructions.
- Provide additional processing time before repeating or rephrasing.
- Check for understanding by asking students to demonstrate rather than just repeat back.

Ensure all team members are using compatible strategies and terminology. If you're working on spatial concepts, make sure the occupational therapist and teacher are using the same vocabulary and approaches.

Establish systems for sharing information about student progress and challenges across settings. What works in the therapy room should be tried in the classroom, and classroom observations should inform therapy planning.

CONCLUSION

Developing strong receptive language skills forms the foundation for all communication success in autistic learners. By understanding the unique ways autism affects language comprehension, implementing evidence-based intervention strategies, and working collaboratively with families and teams, we can help our students build the understanding skills they need to participate fully in their educational and social environments.

Remember that progress may look different for each student, and success should be measured not just by performance on structured tasks but by meaningful improvements in functional communication and participation. Every step toward better comprehension opens doors to greater independence, social connection, and academic achievement.

The strategies outlined in this chapter provide a roadmap for systematic, individualized intervention that honors each student's unique strengths and challenges while building the comprehension skills essential for lifelong communication success. Through patient, persistent, and evidence-based practice, we can help every autistic learner reach their full potential for understanding and engaging with the linguistic world around them.

As you implement these approaches with your students, remain flexible and responsive to their individual needs. What works for one learner may need modification for another. The key is maintaining focus on functional outcomes while using systematic, evidence-based methods to achieve meaningful progress in receptive language development.

Please refer to Appendix A for receptive identification activities.

CHAPTER 7

From Chaos to Progress: Running Effective Groups for Nonspeaking Students

During my second year as a speech therapist at the Cleveland Clinic, I was working with four kindergarten students in their autism program. I had carefully planned what I thought was the perfect group activity: making trail mix using a visual recipe I'd created with Boardmaker symbols, complete with lamination and Velcro pieces.

The session went beautifully. Each student took turns matching their visual icon to the recipe, pouring their assigned ingredient into the bowl. We stirred together, used language, and practiced turn-taking. I was mentally congratulating myself when we reached the best part, trying the trail mix we had just made.

I asked one student if he wanted to try some trail mix. I walked over to offer him some, and without saying a word he took the entire container and flung it toward the ceiling. It was literally raining raisins!

But I learned something crucial that day: Answering yes/no questions is a very complex language skill, and I needed better ways to plan for my emerging communicators. More importantly, I realized that the most effective group activities don't require expensive materials or elaborate setups. Instead, they focus on incorporating literacy and movement in ways that promote genuine peer interaction and communication.

According to ASHA's Autism Practice Portal, the goal of treatment is to improve social communication and modify behaviors so that individuals can develop relationships, function effectively in social situations, and actively participate in everyday life. Group therapy is uniquely positioned to address these core challenges by:

- **Initiating spontaneous communication in functional activities.** Groups provide natural opportunities for students to communicate for real purposes.
- **Engaging in reciprocal communication interactions.** The back-and-forth nature of group activities builds essential social skills.
- **Generalizing skills across activities, environments, and communication partners.** What students learn in group can transfer to classrooms, playgrounds, and home.

In my 20-plus years in the field, I have provided group therapy in schools and clinics. In this chapter I'll share strategies you can use to feel confident in planning fun and functional groups for your students.

Before diving into specific activities, ask yourself these guiding questions:

- **Why am I seeing these students together?** While scheduling constraints are real, we can still make group time functional and meaningful for everyone involved. If you are going into a classroom to provide therapy, ask the teacher for their schedule. Is there a time that you can go into the classroom? Make sure that there will be other team members in the classroom too. Other team members can help with prompting when needed, data collection, etc. It is also a great time for the speech therapist to model how they are working on language for the various students and goals.
- **What shared goals can we work on together?** Look for overlapping IEP objectives around social communication, turn-taking, following group directions, or peer interaction. I have created a data sheet, available in Appendix C. I like to write in the student goals at the start of the year and then make copies so that I can chart data during each session. The data sheet also has a general area where you can write the activities down that you do for the group. Sharing this specific data can be very helpful when you are in meetings or when you are doing progress reports. Including specific information allows us to create a visual picture about what is taking place during our group therapy sessions.
- **How can I make this group beneficial for all students?** At a training many years ago in Austin, Texas, the speaker shared a picture of a shirt her client used to wear. It said, "I have autism" on the front and "Don't waste my time" on the back. I love this! We want to make sure that the groups we lead have a purpose and that everyone has an opportunity to participate.
- **How can I facilitate peer-to-peer interaction?** Your goal is to work yourself out of a job, so students are engaging naturally with each other. This is tough to facilitate at first, but we want to provide prompts that we can systematically fade, if possible. Peer-to-peer interaction can be hard to facilitate at first. We might need to specifically plan on how we will work on this in group, but over time it gets easier, I promise!

For example, if we want to work on greetings, instead of prompting the student to say hi to (Tanner), we could say, "Oh, there is Tanner!" which then prompts the student to say, "Hi, Tanner." We always want to simulate our students naturally engaging with one another. The focus of therapy is to practice social skills that can be generalized across the learner's day.

- **What prompts do my students need, and how can I phase them out?** Use prompts as teaching tools, not permanent supports. That said, some students may always need a prompt for certain skills. It is up to us to really evaluate what supports are needed and if/when they can be faded. Our goal is always student independence with communication.
- **What other adult help do I need?** Having support for prompting, behavior management, and data collection makes a world of difference. Adult support also allows you to model how to work on communication throughout the student's school day.

Now that we have asked some questions to get us up and running, it is time to get into the group framework (Figure 7.1). When we work within a framework, it's win–win

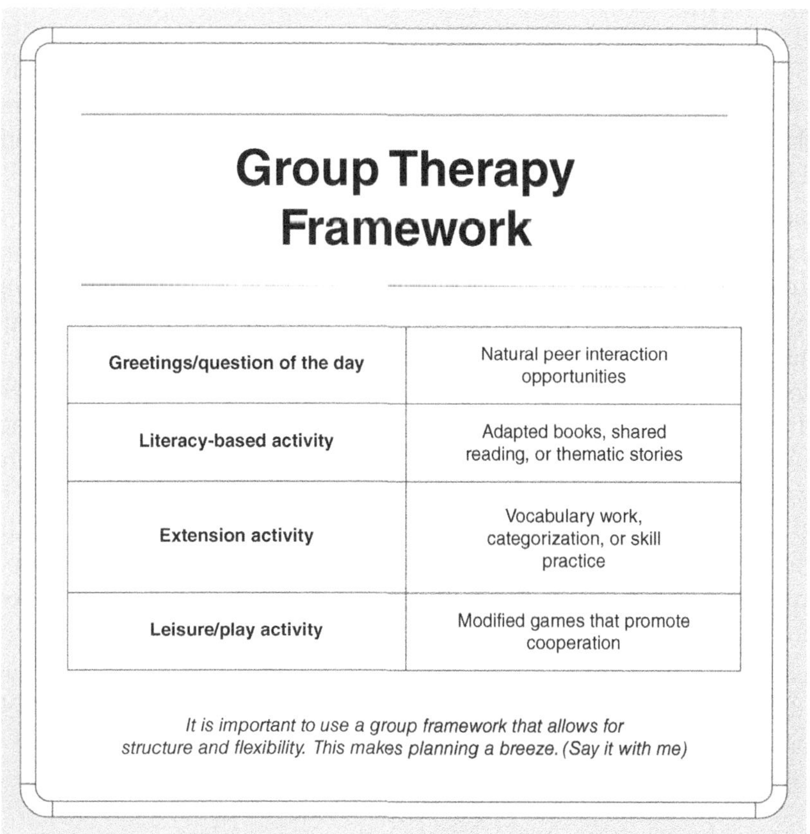

Greetings/question of the day	Natural peer interaction opportunities
Literacy-based activity	Adapted books, shared reading, or thematic stories
Extension activity	Vocabulary work, categorization, or skill practice
Leisure/play activity	Modified games that promote cooperation

FIGURE 7.1 Group therapy framework.

because it's easier to plan for us and our students know what to expect. Regardless of age group, here's my general group framework:

- **Greetings/question of the day**—Natural peer interaction opportunities
- **Literacy-based activity**—Adapted books, shared reading, or thematic stories
- **Extension activity**—Vocabulary work, categorization, or skill practice
- **Leisure/play activity**—Modified games that promote cooperation

This framework is flexible enough to work with preschoolers through high school students while maintaining the core elements that promote social communication. In the remaining sections of the chapter we will discuss specific therapy plans, so that you can use these with your own students.

GROUP ACTIVITY IDEAS

1. Weather Theme

Greeting: Simple "Hi" exchanges between peers. Students can wave, verbalize hello, or use their AAC device to say hi to peers. I don't use the direction, "Say hi to (classmate)." I usually say, "Oh, I see (classmate)!" and then model a greeting. This type of prompting is more natural and mirrors the natural environment.

Literacy-based activity: *Winter Summer* adapted book with real photos. This is an adapted weather book that I created to use with my students. I love to use adapted books with my students! All the adapted books I have created at ABA Speech use real-life pictures. Using real-life pictures is so very important and meaningful for our students. You can grab this in the supplemental materials section for the book over at www.abaspeech. org. I love to show this book on a smartboard when available or on an iPad. When reading this book, I may have the students come up to the board to read a page. Other students may come up to the board and label an item they see from the book with their device. I develop ways for each student to participate in this section of the group. The weather book uses simple text with real photographs, as you can see in Figure 7.1: "In the summer, I like to swim in the pool." "In the winter, I like to go sledding." This book also has two of each picture from the book. These pictures can be used to support labeling, comprehension, and matching skills too.

Extension activity: An extension activity that is fun for this theme is categorizing. I write the words *winter* and *summer* on a classroom dry erase board. We also have laminated pictures that depict items needed or weather related to each season. These words and pictures may include but are not limited to *hat, scarf, flip flops, bathing suit, snow, sun,* *snow pants,* and *shorts.* The students will take turns picking a picture and categorizing it under the season.

Leisure/play activity: Modified Simon Says. Refer to Chapter 4.

2. Farm Theme

Question of the day: Today we are using our Let's Talk Boom card that comes with visuals for our question of the day. Questions could include:

- What is your favorite animal?
- What breakfast food do you like?
- What is your favorite color?

You can also make your own question of the day resource by using Google slides and photographs. Choose one student to go first. That student will come to the smart board or iPad and answer the question; they will choose the next student or you can choose the next student to go (base this on your student's goals). Some of the students I work with have a goal to answer a social question from an adult, some may have a goal to answer a social question when asked by a peer.

Literacy-based activity: *Our Trip to the Farm* adapted book. You can grab this in the supplemental materials section for the book over at www.abaspeech.org. I love to show this book on a smartboard when available or on an iPad. This is another simple adapted book. It has one picture per page and one sentence. We saw a cow and it said _______. This book has a simple fill in the blank sentence on each page with real-life pictures of things you might see on a farm.

Extension activity: For this activity you can do the included fill-in-the-blank phrases for common animals, which are part of the adapted book. A cat says,____________ (meow), A duck says _________ (quack). You could also do a matching activity if you have picture cards depicting farm animals and mini farm animals. You can lay the cards on the table in a messy array and hold up a mini farm animal. You can hand it to the student and give the direction "Match cow," or "Put with cow."

Leisure/play activity: Modified musical chairs. Refer to Chapter 4.

3. Virtual Aquarium Field Trip

I got the idea for virtual field trips during COVID. I was still seeing students five days a week and I wanted to make therapy fun during such a stressful time. Virtual field trips are a great idea for student engagement! This group format is a lesson plan around a virtual field trip to an aquarium.

Question of the day: For our question of the day activity, you can write a timely question. If it is fall, you could ask, "What do you like to do in the fall?" and write three choices with a small rectangular box next to the text. Your choices could be:

- Visit a pumpkin patch.
- Go to a football game.
- See the leaves change colors.

Each student can take a turn putting a tally next to their choice. After they vote, they ask another student, and hand the marker to them.

Literacy-based activity: We will be reading *Trip to the Aquarium*, an adapted book. You can see this in the Supplemental Materials section for the book over at www.abaspeech.org. I love to show this book on a smartboard when available or on an iPad because the pictures are vibrant and engaging. This book is all about taking a trip to the aquarium in a group, so we work on the pronoun *we* in a sentence, such as, "We see a turtle." "We see a jellyfish." Depending on where students live or if they have not been to an aquarium before, this might be good exposure to new vocabulary too.

Extension activity: This is one of my favorite extension activities. For this activity we will visit the Monterey Bay Aquarium via one of their many live web cams. Students can choose which animals they want to see. Our personal favorite is the jellyfish cam! They are so beautiful to look at from afar. During this activity, students can choose by verbalizing, using their device or pointing to the animal they want to see on the live web cam—this is a fun activity for all involved!

Leisure/play activity: Modified Scrabble

1. Using the game Scrabble, students can place their tiles on the holder or can put them face up or face down on the desk.
2. In our modified version, students will take turns making words on the board, but the words do not have to connect.
3. If your student would benefit from more support, grab a small dry erase board and help them develop a word they can create for their turn. Show them the word and have them create the word on the Scrabble board.

4. Pizza Party

Question of the day: For our question of the day activity, try a trivia question. This could be a question about a favorite teacher or someone in the school. For example: "What is Mrs. Smith's (classroom teacher) favorite sport to watch?" Write the question on the board and put three potential answers. Each student would take a turn putting a tally next to their choice. After they vote or at the end of the group, the answer is revealed.

Literacy-based activity: For our pizza party theme we read *Pete the Cat and the Perfect Pizza Party*. When you open the book, before you even start reading there are pizzas with all sorts of silly toppings—like a fish, an apple, dirt, and even eggs. My students love to point out all the yucky and unexpected toppings they see. It is all about Pete and his friends making a pizza. They put a lot of nontraditional toppings on the pizza and then they all try it!

Extension activity: For this extension activity we like to play a category game. You can see this in the Supplemental Materials section for the book over at www.abaspeech.org. This is a fun word game that pairs nicely with this book. Name five breakfast foods, name five vehicles, etc.

Leisure/play activity: Grocery Store Game (YouTube video model available)

This is a fun alphabet game (Figure 7.2).

1. In this game we take turns thinking of a food or item that we can buy at the grocery store.
2. Write the first letter of half the alphabet on a dry erase board. You can do the entire alphabet, but I find that takes too long, so I break it up.
3. Explain you are going to take turns thinking of a food item or item that we can buy from the grocery store that starts with each letter of the alphabet.
4. Demonstrate by taking a turn first. "A is for apple."
5. Take turns developing words. If you have a dry erase board, you can write the developed words out.
6. Use visuals if your student needs help developing a word. We have a printable in the supplemental materials that you can use! It has a visual for each letter of the alphabet.

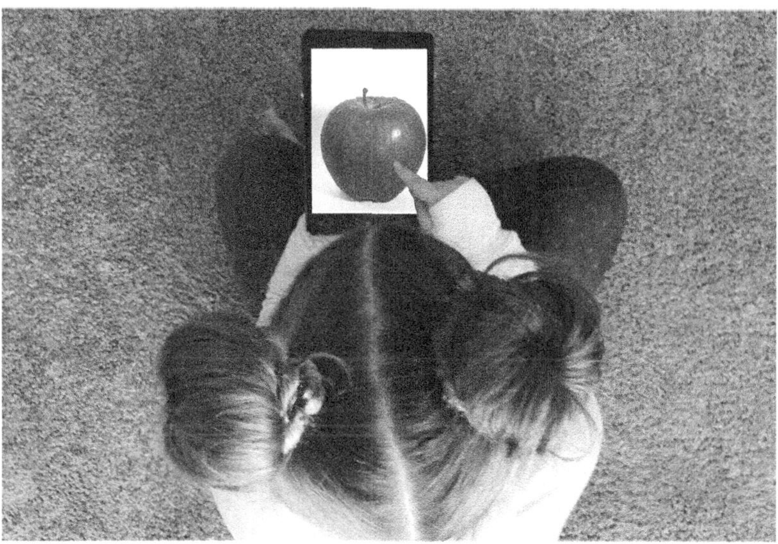

FIGURE 7.2   Grocery store game.

5. Vocational Skills

I spent many years running a vocational group with a special education teacher and occupational therapist. From that experience, I created a vocational binder that includes 15 units. Restaurant, housekeeping, retail, and landscape are some of the units included. Each unit has a literacy-based activity, a vocabulary section, comprehension questions, social language questions, and extension activities that allow students to get the opportunity to practice work skills associated with the various units that are discussed. The key is connecting what you practice in a group to what students will encounter in their actual vocational training or community experiences.

Question of the day: We would tie our question on the day into the vocational unit that we are learning about. For example, if the unit we are addressing is grocery store, our question of the day may be, "What department or role would you want to work in?" Dairy, produce, bagger? The students who are participating in the group would take turns answering this question. This is a fun way to kick off the session.

Literacy-based activity: There are 15 units in the vocational binder. The housekeeping unit is a free unit, and you can get access to this with the supplemental book materials. It discusses what it might look like to work in housekeeping. Every group is different; for some groups, we may take turns reading the passage, and for other groups I may read the passage to them.

Extension activity: The vocational binder and the free unit that you will have access to all have their own built in extension activities! For housekeeping guidance on jobs that students can practice are included. Students can learn how to vacuum, learn how to spray cleaner with a spray bottle and wipe the table, etc.

Leisure/play activity: Weightlifting with Water Bottles or Group Yoga

Weightlifting with Water Bottles

I always wanted to be an aerobics instructor, so this part of the group is me living my dream!

1. Each student has a bag with their name on it and two closed water bottles.
2. The students grab their bag and get their water bottle weights out.
3. The instructor (the SLP for our purposes today) stands in front of the class and models an exercise, perhaps bicep curls. They do 10 reps and have the students do it too.
4. Repeat with other exercises.
5. We usually listen to music too!

Group Yoga

1. Tell the students, "Okay, we are going to do yoga."
2. Dim the lights if possible.

3. Model standing poses for the students and have them do it after you (My OT had a nice deck of yoga cards. I have also just used Google images to create large, laminated pictures of various standing poses.)
4. Enjoy!

DELIVERY OPTIONS

Before we wrap up this chapter, I wanted to share the various ways that group therapy can be delivered. If I know one thing, it is that the schedule of a therapist is full and always changing!

SLP Runs Group in Classroom

This is my personal favorite. You go into the general education or special education classroom and run your group there. Benefits include:

- Natural environment for generalization
- Teacher can observe and continue strategies
- Students remain in familiar setting
- Easier to incorporate classroom themes/curriculum

Planning considerations:
- Who will be in the group and when?
- How will you incorporate individual student goals?
- What support staff will be available?
- How will you take data?
- Can you co-treat with other professionals?

SLP and Teacher or Related-service Providers Co-treat

This requires planning time but can be incredibly effective.

Example: The Mitten Activity
- Read *The Mitten* together (teacher handles reading)
- SLP station: "Mitten Adventure" where students find mittens hiding their individual labeling targets around the room
- Teacher station: Matching colored mittens by design and pattern
- Students rotate between stations, working on both labeling and visual discrimination

Planning considerations:

- What skills will be addressed by each professional?
- What role will each person play?
- How will you coordinate data collection?
- What materials does each person provide?

SLP as Consultant and Coach

Sometimes the most impactful work happens through consultation.

Example: Morning meeting support. A teacher requested help with a student who couldn't participate in daily morning meeting. The student had no way to communicate during calendar time, weather discussions, or group songs.

Solution: We created a *Morning Meeting Book* with visuals for all the routine activities. I worked on it with the student during individual therapy sessions, then went into the classroom to model its use and coach the teacher and paraprofessionals on implementation.

Planning considerations:

- When is the best time to observe?
- How does the teacher prefer to receive feedback?
- Can you set up a shared Google Doc for ongoing communication?
- How will you let parents know about your classroom support?

DATA KEEPING

Now that we have our group lesson ready to go and our delivery options laid out, let's talk data. Keeping data is crucial so we can demonstrate progress and make decisions about future treatment targets. Keep it simple but systematic:

- Track participation frequency for each student.
- Note prompting levels needed for group instructions.
- Document peer interactions (initiated vs. responded).
- Record specific IEP goal progress.
- Use quick notation systems (tally marks, +/– systems).

Consider having support staff help with data collection so you can focus on facilitation and teaching.

Troubleshooting Common Challenges

"My students have very different language levels." Use the same framework but differentiate within activities. During question of the day, one student might point to a visual while another gives a full sentence response. Both are participating meaningfully.

"I don't have time to make materials." Focus on activities that require minimal preparation. Use books you already have, create simple visual supports, and repurpose classroom games. The relationships and interactions matter more than fancy materials.

"Students aren't interacting with each other." Start with structured peer interactions ("Ask Sarah what her favorite color is") and gradually fade your facilitation. It takes time to build these skills.

"Behavior challenges make group difficult." Ensure you have adequate support, use visual schedules for group activities, and consider whether all students are appropriately placed in the group. Sometimes individual work is needed before group success is possible.

Here's a secret from 20 years of group therapy: *Use the same framework for three weeks in a row.* For instance:

- **Week 1:** Students learn the routine and get comfortable.
- **Week 2:** Students participate more actively as familiarity increases.
- **Week 3:** Students are fully engaged and demonstrate their best social communication skills.

Then you can introduce a new theme or framework. This repetition builds confidence and allows students to focus on communication rather than figuring out what's expected.

My goal in group therapy is to work myself out of a job. I want students naturally interacting, supporting each other, and enjoying shared activities without constant adult facilitation.

Signs of Success

- Students greet each other without prompts.
- Peer-to-peer conversations happen spontaneously.
- Students help each other during activities.
- Natural play and leisure interactions emerge.
- Skills generalize to other settings.

Remember Jan, who threw the trail mix? By the end of that school year, he was one of my most engaged group participants. He would always greet me with "Hi, Miss Rose!" when I entered the room to set up for group therapy.

The trail mix incident taught me that our students are always communicating—*we just need to create better frameworks for understanding and supporting their communication attempts.* Group therapy, when done thoughtfully and systematically, provides the perfect opportunities for building these essential life skills.

CONCLUSION

Group therapy for autistic students isn't just about addressing IEP goals—*it's about building the foundation for lifelong relationships, community participation, and social joy.* By using a consistent framework, incorporating students' interests, and systematically building peer interaction skills, we can create groups that students genuinely look forward to attending.

The specific examples and frameworks in this chapter have been tested with hundreds of students over two decades of practice. They work because they're based on what we know about autism, social communication development, and effective instruction. More importantly, they're designed to be sustainable for busy professionals while remaining engaging and meaningful for students.

Start with one group. Use the framework. Give it three weeks. Watch the magic happen when students begin connecting with each other in ways that extend far beyond your therapy room.

After all, isn't that why we do this work? Not for perfect data sheets or flawless IEP goal mastery but for those moments when we see our students building relationships, enjoying shared experiences, and participating fully in their world. Group therapy, done right, creates exactly those opportunities.

CHAPTER 8

Supporting Students with Behavioral Barriers

One of my closest friends owns an ABA agency here in my hometown in Ohio. Before I started ABA Speech, I worked in her agency part time. Her agency offers a school for students who have behavioral barriers that make it difficult for them to attend a public school. One of the students I worked with for three years came to our school at the age of 10. He had no way to communicate, despite having a perfectly set up AAC device. Let's call him "Nate." Nate engaged in not only aggressive behavior to others, but he also engaged in self-injurious behaviors. When he entered the program, he worked in a small classroom with his materials and his 1:1 instructors. He worked in this way, to keep himself and other students and staff safe.

I would go to see him for speech therapy twice a week in 30-minute sessions. Our first sessions were focused on building rapport and getting to know what he liked to do for fun. I slowly phased in some structured teaching of requesting his favorite things using his AAC device. He loved the mini trampoline, taking sensory breaks, and listening to music. I had his 1:1 technician with us for safety and so that I could model how to work on communication.

Nate's first IEP focused on joint attention, care of his device (remembering to grab it before he left the room, carrying it around the school, etc.), and requesting and receptive identification of preferred and common nouns and actions. Once Nate was given very robust and intense ABA and speech therapy services, he was able to start using his device on his own. It was amazing to see the transformation take place!

After about six months in the program, we had the opportunity to take the kids to Dairy Queen. We had practiced how he would order with his AAC device for about two weeks before we went. On the day of the field trip, he waited in line with his 1:1 tech and when the cashier asked him, "What do you want?" he oriented to his device to say, "Chicken fingers and fries." Wow!! What a moment. I could not believe that it took Nate 10 years to find his voice, but when he found it, he felt empowered and confident.

Working with Nate was intimidating at first due to his challenging behavior, but having a structure that would allow Nate to learn at school was vital to his success. Working in the school environment can make this even more difficult. But no matter what setting you work in, the information in this chapter will help you feel empowered to help all students.

DECODING BEHAVIOR

When students engage in challenging behaviors during therapy sessions, our first instinct might be frustration, confusion, or even fear. However, these behaviors are rarely random. They serve a purpose for the student, even when that purpose isn't immediately clear to us. Understanding the "why" behind behavior is the foundation of effective support.

Behavior typically occurs due to one or more of the four functions:

1. **Attention.** Problem behavior often results in immediate attention through head turns, attempts to soothe, or redirection. For students who struggle to gain attention through appropriate means, challenging behavior becomes an effective communication strategy.

   Example: A student might engage in self-injurious behavior when the teacher's attention shifts to another student, knowing this will immediately bring adult focus back to them.

2. **Access to preferred items or activities.** Many behaviors result in accessing preferred items, activities, or sensory experiences. When students lack the communication skills to appropriately request what they want, behavior becomes their request system.

   Example: A student might cry or have a meltdown until their preferred activity (like watching a specific video) is provided.

3. **Automatic or self-stimulatory.** Some behaviors don't depend on others' responses because they directly produce their own reinforcement. These behaviors often serve a sensory function, providing input that feels good or regulating the student's nervous system.

   Example: A student might repeatedly flip through pages of a book not to read but because the tactile sensation and visual stimulation feel satisfying.

4. **Escape/avoidance.** Behaviors can be learned as effective ways to terminate or postpone unwanted events, tasks, or interactions. For students who feel overwhelmed or lack the skills for a particular demand, challenging behavior becomes their way of saying, "I need a break."

   Example: A student might engage in aggressive behavior whenever academic demands are presented, leading adults to remove the demands and provide a break.

ABC DATA COLLECTION

To truly understand why behavior occurs, we need to become behavioral detectives. This involves systematic observation using ABC data collection—tracking the Antecedent (what happened before), Behavior (what exactly occurred), and Consequence (what happened after).

Antecedent: The environmental events, instructions, or conditions that occur immediately before the behavior. This might include:

- Transition announcements
- Presentation of nonpreferred tasks
- Changes in routine
- Sensory triggers (loud noises, bright lights)
- Social situations

Behavior: The observable, measurable action the student takes. This should be described objectively without interpretation:

- "Student threw iPad across the room" rather than "Student had a tantrum."
- "Student hit peer on the arm three times" rather than "Student was aggressive."

Consequence: The response from the environment immediately following the behavior. This includes:

- Adult responses (attention, comfort, redirection)
- Peer reactions
- Environmental changes (removal from situation, access to preferred items)
- Natural outcomes

When we collect ABC data consistently, patterns emerge that help us understand the function of behavior. We might discover that challenging behaviors primarily occur:

- During specific activities or with certain staff members
- At particular times of day
- When specific demands are presented
- In certain environments or settings

This information becomes invaluable for developing effective intervention strategies.

At times we may have team members who are available to help us understand the why of this behavior. Other times we may not! Using the chart included will allow you to see if there is a pattern to the behavior. Perhaps you go to the classroom to get the student for speech therapy, but they have been on their iPad for 25 minutes. Or maybe you see a student right at the end of the day and they are sleepy, or you could see a student on a day that they have a substitute teacher or tech. There are many reasons that problem behavior may occur. If we don't log it we will not know how to support our students effectively. I have included the ABC data chart as a helpful resource in Appendix D, Functional Behavioral Assessments.

When behavior significantly impacts a student's learning or safety, a Functional Behavior Assessment (FBA) may be warranted. An FBA uses both direct observation and indirect methods (interviews, rating scales) to identify the function of challenging behavior.

Who typically conducts FBAs:

- School psychologists
- Board Certified Behavior Analysts (BCBAs)
- Special education teachers with behavioral expertise
- Teams of professionals working collaboratively

The FBA process results in a comprehensive understanding of why behavior occurs, which then informs the development of a Behavior Intervention Plan (BIP) with specific strategies for prevention, teaching, and response. In my experience, the BIP is included with the Individual Education Plan (IEP). As a treating SLP, you will want to make sure that you have access to each student's BIP. Having access to this plan will help you understand strategies to use antecedently so that problem behavior does not occur, and it will also help you feel more comfortable with how to proceed if it does occur.

If you support a student who engages in behavior that is a barrier to their therapy sessions you should ask the teacher if the student has a behavior intervention plan. If they do, get the plan. If they do not, discuss with the team requesting an FBA. A student's behavior is communicating something, and it is up to us to advocate for them.

Supporting students with behavioral challenges requires thoughtful consideration of multiple factors that can make or break the success of our interventions. We want to create a safe and successful environment. Feeling safe at work is key. If you don't feel safe at work, tell someone. This may look like you going into the classroom to provide therapy so that other adults are close by. You could also provide therapy in your office with a paraprofessional or 1:1 technician coming with the student to provide behavioral support.

The location and structure of therapy sessions can significantly impact behavior. Consider the possible options.

THERAPY LOCATION CONSIDERATIONS

Service	Pros	Cons	Best for...
Classroom	Natural environment, potential for peer interaction, support from classroom staff	Possible distractions, multiple adults, less control over environment	Students who benefit from natural contexts and need more intense behavioral support
Therapy Room	Controlled environment, fewer distractions, individualized attention	Less natural, potential for difficulty transitioning; may need staff to attend sessions as well	Students who need minimal distractions and highly structured environments
Larger School Environment	Hallways, libraries, outdoor spaces, or other settings may provide the optimal learning environment for some students	The key is individualizing based on student needs and goals	A great way to plan for the generalization of skills

Determining the location of therapy is important for our safety and the safety of the student. (Say It With Me)

When we are planning intervention for a student, especially those with IEPs, thinking about service location prior to the IEP meeting is key. With an IEP, we need to specify where the student will receive the service. If I see a student one hour a week, I may split that up to a 30-minute individual session in my office with a technician present and a 30-minute group therapy session in the classroom. Alternatively, I might split that up into a 30-minute 1:1 session in the classroom and a 30-minute session with paraprofessional support in the larger school environment. These are just examples based on specific student needs.

STAFF SUPPORT

I have extensive experience working in both the clinical and school environment. Having the support of technicians, RBTs (registered behavioral technicians) and paraprofessionals can be vital when providing therapy.

One-to-One Support

When available, paraprofessionals or RBTs can provide invaluable assistance with these tasks:

- Implement behavior plans consistently.
- Collect data during sessions.
- Ensure safety for all participants.
- Support generalization of skills.

Training and Communication

All staff working with the student should:

- Understand the behavior intervention plan.
- Know their specific roles and responsibilities.
- Receive training on specific strategies.
- Have access to ongoing support and consultation.

MATERIALS

We also need to be organized in this area to feel at peace and calm during sessions:

- Have all materials organized and immediately accessible.
- Prepare backup activities for students who struggle to engage in therapy tasks.
- Anticipate potential triggers and having alternatives ready.
- Maintain engagement to prevent behavioral momentum loss.

In our trainings in the ABA Speech Connection, I share that taking time upfront to organize and have materials ready is a good investment. One hack is to use a large organizer with file folders labeled with the student's IEP goals and objectives. Inside the file folders, put any visual materials that are needed to work on that target. For example, if objective 1.3 is to label familiar people, we may have a variety of pictures of our student's family members, teachers, and classmates. So that when our student is ready to work on that objective, we are prepared in advance.

Visuals in general can help our students feel more comfortable with the flow of therapy. Visuals may include daily schedules, mini therapy schedules, choice boards, or anything that will be helpful for your learner.

Visuals can provide:

- Predictability and structure
- Support for communication and understanding
- Reduced anxiety about unknown expectations
- Clear pathways for making choices

Other visual strategies that may be helpful for your student include the following.

Power Cards

Power cards should be quick to implement (30 seconds before challenging situations) and high fidelity (easy for staff to implement correctly). Create individualized cards featuring the student's special interests (dinosaurs, *Frozen* characters, *Pokémon*) with two to three behavioral expectations written from the character's perspective:

- "T-Rex keeps his hands to himself on the playground."
- "Elsa stays in her castle where she's safe" (for a student who runs away).

Visual Behavior Plans

Transform text-heavy behavior plans into visual flowcharts showing:

- When to implement strategies
- Clear connections between prevention, teaching, and response strategies
- Step-by-step instructions with illustrations
- Easy-to-follow decision trees for different scenarios

When supporting students who engage in behavior that is a barrier to their learning, we must be mindful and compassionate about how we discuss this behavior. Our language sets the tone and culture of the services that we provide. When possible do not talk about the student in front of the student. We do need to inform staff to keep everyone safe but be mindful of how this is being done. Being respectful of our students is vital in providing compassionate services.

STRENGTH-BASED LANGUAGE EXAMPLES

Deficit-based language	Strength-based language
"She is obsessed."	"She is passionate."
"He is bouncing off the walls!"	"He is high energy!"
"She is off in her own world."	"She is internally focused."
"He is so rigid."	"He values consistency."

Our words matter. Advocating for the use of strength-based language sets a culture of compassionate care.

EASY, EASY, HARD STRATEGY

A specific and effective intervention is the **Easy, Easy, Hard Strategy**. This strategy helps our students feel successful and allows them to work on more difficult skills with confidence.

- Begin with two to three skills the student can do easily.
- Build behavioral momentum before presenting more challenging activities.
- See some examples in the following table.

	Preschool	School-age
Easy	SLP: (holds up a familiar animal toy) Student: "Dog." SLP: "It is a dog."	SLP: "Ready, Set, ____" Student: "Go." SLP: "Wow, awesome filing in the blank."
Easy	SLP: (holds up a picture of the student's mom) "Mama" Student: "Mama."	SLP: (holds up a picture of a person reading a book) "What's happening in this picture?" Student: "Reading." SLP: "Yes, he is reading."
Hard	SLP: "What is your first name?" Student: (Pauses for two seconds) "Bubba." SLP: "Wow, Bubba, great working."	SLP lays out three cards (a bike, a kite and a marshmallow) and says, "Which one do you ride?" The student points to bike SLP: Yes, you ride a bike!

When you implement this into your own therapy sessions, it is a good idea to keep a running list of skills that your student can easily accomplish. You can use the skills chart in Appendix A to help with this.

CASE STUDY: NATE'S COMPREHENSIVE SUPPORT IN ACTION

Remember Nate, the student I talked about at the start of the chapter? I want to tell you more about his comprehensive plan. Recall that he was an eight-year-old autistic student who had no functional communication and used aggressive behavior that prevented him from accessing the community and education. I worked with him in a specialized educational setting.

Interventions

Nate's intervention involved:

Assessment and Planning

- Informal communication assessments
- VB-MAPP evaluation by outside BCBA
- Collaborative goal development across disciplines (teacher, SLP, BCBA, OT)

Service Delivery Modifications

- Therapy provided in his individual classroom space
- One-to-one staff support during all sessions
- 30-minute session durations based on his overall engagement

Coordinated Team Approach

- Shared data collection across all staff
- Weekly meetings with support staff
- Monthly consultation with BCBA
- Training provided to all team members on communication strategies

Outcomes

Over time, Nate's unsafe behavior decreased, and his communication increased! Watching him use his AAC device to order food at Dairy Queen was just one of the amazing transformations. We also saw him participating in main classroom activities, using his AAC device functionally across the day, significant reduction in aggressive behaviors, and his family was able to operate safely at home, including visits from grandma and grandpa (which had been stopped prior to his coming to the specialized program). As practitioners, we likely all have a Nate in our lives, and to be able to see this growth and change is why I do what I do every day at ABA Speech!

So, if you are supporting students currently who engage in behavior that is a barrier to therapy, remember to take these steps:

1. **Conduct ABC observations** to identify behavioral patterns.
2. **Analyze current service delivery** to determine optimal settings and supports.
3. **Ensure access to behavior plans** and understand all team members' roles.
4. **Prepare materials thoroughly** to maintain engagement and prevent behavioral escalation.
5. **Advocate for appropriate support** when safety or learning is compromised.
6. **Use visual supports** to improve understanding and recall of behavioral strategies.
7. **Focus on collaborative decision-making** rather than top-down directive approaches.
8. **Regularly review and adjust** strategies based on data and team feedback.
9. **Foster collaborative relationships** between general education, special education, and related service providers.
10. **Check in with parents regularly** to keep the lines of communication open!

CONCLUSION

Behavioral challenges need not remain mysterious barriers to learning. When we approach these situations with curiosity rather than frustration, systematic observation rather than assumptions, and collaborative problem-solving rather than punitive responses, we can transform both our own experience and our students' outcomes.

Nate's story taught important lessons about the complexity of communication, the importance of preparation, and the need to understand our students' perspectives. But more importantly, it illustrated that even our most challenging moments can become stepping stones toward more effective, compassionate practice.

Every student and therapist deserves to feel safe, understood, and successful in their learning environment. The goal is not to eliminate all challenging behaviors, but to understand their function and teach more effective alternatives while creating environments where all students can thrive.

When we commit to this approach, we don't just help individual students—we contribute to a more inclusive, understanding, and effective educational system for everyone.

CHAPTER 9

AAC Without the Overwhelm: A Practical Guide to Getting Started Today

I will never forget my first job in a specialized autism program in a rural part of Ohio. It was an amazing program where local districts would send their learners who needed more support to be successful in the public school system. I was the speech therapist, and I had an assistant who would also help with all things Augmentative and Alternative Communication (AAC). This was my first time working with dynamic speech-generating devices, and I was terrified! I had no clue how to navigate the vocabulary, and I used my assistant's confidence in AAC to let me dodge really digging in for about a month. After a month I could no longer handle feeling ineffective, so I took an hour and really dove into the AAC vocabulary my students were using. After that time, I felt silly that I let an AAC device make me feel so inadequate.

So, if you feel less than confident in supporting students who use AAC or students who might be a good candidate for AAC—STOP! You can do this, and this chapter will be a great first step. If you are a veteran therapist, you can learn a new strategy or about a new assessment to start using now.

When I was working in that specialized program, I met Timmy, and his journey really showed me the power of AAC. I first met him when he was 10 years old. Timmy didn't talk and engaged in very unsafe behavior that was a barrier to him accessing his local public school. He was also not able to visit family or be in the community. Timmy was frustrated by not being able to communicate. However, he did have an augmentative communication device. It was set up very nicely from his home district, but he did not know how to use it. His parents and teachers were frustrated too. As a speech-language pathologist and board-certified behavior analyst, I was contacted to help him. I met together with a team of others, including Timmy's parents, teachers, and an intervention specialist to develop a plan by which he would be able to functionally use his device across a variety of settings.

First, I established rapport with Timmy by finding out what items and activities he most enjoyed. We found that jumping on a trampoline, listening to music, and watching movies on his iPad were among his favorite activities. I then added these activities to his device so that he could be taught to request some throughout the day whenever he desired. I made sure that the other members of his team were present during treatment sessions so that I could model how to work on communication. We agreed to keep data on Timmy's use of his device and to meet weekly to compare his progress. It was amazing to see his growth! His unsafe behavior decreased as his ability to use his AAC device increased. I hated that Timmy had to wait 10 years to communicate on his own, but once he started, he was unstoppable!

This chapter explores the fundamentals of AAC, drawing from both foundational knowledge and cutting-edge research to provide practitioners with comprehensive guidance for assessment, intervention, and collaboration. We examine how understanding typical development can inform AAC target selection, explore methods for determining learner preferences beyond simple item requests, and discuss strategies for expanding communication beyond basic requesting to include varied word classes and pragmatic functions. In addition, I have included activities that you can use with your students and some of the goals included in our AAC goal bank in the ABA Speech Connection.

BEYOND WORDS

Augmentative and Alternative Communication represents an area of clinical practice that supplements or compensates for impairments in speech-language production. The field recognizes that communication extends far beyond spoken words and encompasses multiple modalities and systems designed to meet individual needs. It should also be noted that AAC can and should be used when appropriate for students who verbally communicate. I have used AAC with students who are not verbal communicators and those who are verbal communicators but who also supplement their speech with an AAC device.

AAC systems are typically divided into two broad categories: unaided and aided communication. Unaided AAC does not require any external tool and includes body language, facial expressions, finger spelling, gestures, manual signs, vocalizations, and verbalizations. These forms of communication rely entirely on the individual's body and can be immediately accessible in most environments.

Aided AAC, in contrast, requires some form of external tool, either electronic or nonelectronic. Nonelectronic aided forms are often referred to as light-tech or low-tech AAC. These might include communication boards with pictures or symbols, visual schedules, objects, photographs, and writing systems. Electronic forms, known as high-tech AAC, encompass computer-based systems, tablets with AAC software, smartphones with communication apps, speech-generating devices, and various assistive technologies.

The spectrum of AAC options reflects the diversity of communication needs across individuals. Some students may benefit from simple picture exchange systems, while others require sophisticated speech-generating devices with dynamic symbol language representation and text-to-speech features. The key lies in matching the system to the individual's specific needs, preferences, and capabilities.

Before we get into my favorite and free AAC assessment tool, it's important to review the *Communication Bill of Rights*, which was published in 1992 by the National Joint Committee for the Communication Needs of Persons with Severe Disabilities (NJC). It establishes that every person, regardless of the extent of their disability, has the following rights:

1. The right to dignity and respect in all interactions
2. The right to meaningful communication that is culturally and linguistically appropriate
3. The right to be addressed directly and not be spoken for or talked about as if not there
4. The right to receive a response to all communication, even when the desired outcome is not possible
5. The right to participate across settings as full communication partners
6. The right to interact socially and to build and keep relationships
7. The right to be given—and to understand—information about objects, actions, events, and people
8. The right to ask for or refuse objects, actions, events, and people
9. The right to express preferences and feelings, make comments, and share opinions
10. The right to make choices from meaningful options
11. The right to access services and supports for communication across the lifespan
12. The right to individualized, working augmentative and alternative communication (AAC) systems and other assistive technology (AT) at all times

This framework serves as both a philosophical foundation and a practical guide for AAC implementation. It reminds practitioners, families, and educational teams that AAC devices are not optional accessories but essential tools for human connection and self-expression.

Assessment

Assessment in AAC is an ongoing process that extends far beyond initial device selection. The goal is to determine the system components that will optimize communication for the user while recognizing that assessment continues throughout the implementation process.

The Assessment of Learning Partners (ALP) for AAC provides a structured framework for understanding progression in AAC access and learning. This comprehensive assessment tool contains three broad stages of learning with eight specific phases, examining five key areas to determine a learner's current stage and phase:[1]

Stage 1 focuses on body and access method, emphasizing early exposure to the access method through games and participation activities. This stage represents the learner's initial introduction to the AAC system.

Stage 2 incorporates body, access method, and communication, introducing the speech-generating device as a tool for language and communication. This is often when learners experience the "light bulb moment" of understanding that their actions on the device produce meaningful results.

Stage 3 encompasses body, access method, communication, environment, and everyday activities, focusing on improved use and language development within the system.

The ALP examines five key areas:

1. **Activity and movement**—Progressing from seemingly random movements to clear, fluid control of the access method
2. **Understanding**—Developing from no understanding to complete comprehension of the system
3. **Attention**—Moving from distractible to sustained attention during AAC use
4. **Interaction and communication**—Evolving from little or no social interaction to fully integrated communication
5. **Expressions and emotion**—Advancing from neutral responses to independent, situationally appropriate emotional expression

This comprehensive assessment approach recognizes that AAC learning is multifaceted and requires evaluation across multiple domains to create effective intervention plans.

The ALP is a great first start with AAC assessment. Some districts and clinical organizations that I support at ABA Speech have an AAC consultant or AAC contact who may help with the AAC assessment process. Each member on the team may help to collect data during the trial process. A general rule of thumb is to try three AAC devices or three AAC applications to determine which is the best fit for the user.

Another popular AAC assessment is the DAGG-3. The DAGG-3 is located on the Tobii Dynavox website. It helps SLPs collaborate with their clients' teams to assess their current communication abilities. It then provides guidance for choosing and tracking appropriate goals. It is also available free of charge.[2]

Feature matching is also a critical part of the AAC assessment process. We look at what features in an AAC choice are important. When we use feature matching, we are determining the skills and needs of the communicator, identifying the key features needed for effective communication and matching the identified variables with the equipment and resources available.

A robust assessment is important to assure that the correct device and/or application are recommended for a client. Barb Weber, a dually certified SLP/BCBA, led a wonderful course for us in the ABA Speech Connection about AAC assessment. This is a CEU course for both SLPs and BCBAs. This assessment process is so very important because it is one step in right direction to assure that device abandonment does not happen.

Device abandonment occurs when an individual stops using an AAC device despite ongoing need. This occurs in approximately one-third of cases, even when systems are well-designed and functional. Understanding and preventing abandonment requires attention to several key factors:

- **Respect for user choice**—AAC users must have agency in their communication choices. Systems that feel imposed rather than empowering are more likely to be abandoned.
- **Making it fun and functional**—AAC implementation should emphasize enjoyable, meaningful communication opportunities rather than drill-based instruction.
- **Comprehensive team training**—Everyone interacting with the AAC user needs training and ongoing support. This includes family members, educational staff, paraprofessionals, and community members.
- **Device care planning**—Practical considerations such as charging schedules, backup plans, and repair protocols must be established and maintained.
- **Ongoing support**—AAC implementation requires sustained support beyond initial training, including troubleshooting, vocabulary updates, and skill development.

Vocabulary

Traditional AAC vocabulary selection has focused heavily on the distinction between core and fringe vocabulary. Core words are high-frequency words that occur across contexts and speakers, while fringe vocabulary consists of words that are specific to particular contexts or individuals.

However, recent research has challenged the assumption that beginning communicators should start with core vocabulary. Studies examining the MacArthur-Bates Communicative Development Inventories reveal that early communicators—those developing their first 50 words—primarily use what would be classified as fringe vocabulary. These early words include:

- Animal names and sounds
- Vehicles and transportation
- Toys and play items
- Foods and drinks
- People and places
- Body parts
- Environmental objects

This research suggests that for beginning AAC users, a heavy emphasis on fringe vocabulary may be more developmentally appropriate and motivating than starting with abstract core words. The solution is not an either-or approach but rather a balanced strategy that recognizes the developmental progression from concrete, motivating vocabulary to more abstract language concepts.

Moving beyond basic item requests requires understanding what motivates individual learners and building intervention around these preferences. This approach shifts from extrinsic motivation ("She'll give me more play time if I use AAC") to intrinsic motivation ("I'm going to tell her this silly joke using my AAC"). Vocabulary selection was covered more in depth in a journal article course in the ABA Speech Connection.[3]

The following research was discussed in our best-selling course Motivation Matters from Dr. Cindy Gevarter Ph.D. BCBA-D in the ABA Speech Connection. Understanding typical language development patterns informs AAC intervention sequencing. Kathy Binger and colleagues have proposed a *four-phase model of AAC language development* that parallels natural speech development:[4]

Phase 1: Early symbol productions. This phase focuses on building vocabulary and understanding word meanings while developing early pragmatic functions like requesting, rejecting, and basic commenting.

Phase 2: Early symbol combinations. Phase 2 introduces simple, two-word combinations with emerging semantic relations. Word order may not be accurate, but meaning is conveyed through symbol combinations.

Phase 3: Child-like sentences. The next phase emphasizes accurate syntax development with proper word order and the beginning of grammatical complexity.

Phase 4: Adult-like sentences. The last phase involves sophisticated grammar with complex sentence structures and advanced pragmatic functions.

This developmental framework helps practitioners avoid the common mistake of rushing to complex sentence structures before establishing adequate single-word vocabulary and simple combinations.

Before moving to multi-symbol messages, learners benefit from expanding their single-symbol repertoire across different word classes and communicative functions. Single-symbol word classes include:

- **Action words.** Building vocabulary around preferred activities such as "jump," "spin," "squeeze," or "go" provides immediate motivation for communication.
- **Descriptive words.** Children often have strong preferences for specific attributes (big vs. little, red vs. blue) that can drive descriptor vocabulary development.
- **Social words.** Early social vocabulary might include "hi," "bye," and other interaction words that facilitate social connection.

- **Sound effects.** Animal sounds and environmental sounds can be highly motivating and provide natural opportunities for commenting and labeling.
- **Rejection vocabulary.** Teaching "no," "stop," "all done," and other rejection words is crucial for self-advocacy and represents an important early communicative function.

Creating natural opportunities for communication requires strategic environmental manipulation and the use of communication temptations or structured situations that elicit specific communicative responses such as the following:

- **Wrong item format.** Deliberately providing a nonpreferred version of a requested item (green train instead of preferred red train) creates opportunities for descriptor use.
- **Routine interruption.** Starting a preferred activity and then stopping creates natural opportunities for action requests (e.g., pausing during a favorite song to elicit "sing").
- **Delayed assistance.** Providing items that require help (closed containers, turned-off devices) creates opportunities for requesting assistance using words like "open" or "help."
- **Silly situations.** Creating unexpected or amusing scenarios (putting shoes on your head, covering water table with a blanket) can elicit corrective language and location words.
- **Choice opportunities.** Presenting choices between different attributes of the same item type (big dinosaur vs. little dinosaur) naturally elicits descriptor vocabulary.[5]

These strategies work because they create genuine communication needs within motivating contexts, moving away from artificial drill-and-practice approaches toward functional communication instruction.

The transition to multi-symbol communication should be guided by motivational factors and developmental appropriateness. Rather than immediately introducing carrier phrases like "I want," which add little semantic information, practitioners should focus on meaningful semantic relations.

- **Agent + Action:** "Mommy go," "Daddy jump."
- **Action + Object:** "Throw ball," "Eat cookie."
- **Possessor + Possession:** "Mommy's car," "my book."
- **Attribute + Object:** "Big dinosaur," "red car."
- **Location Relations:** "In box," "on table."

These early combinations provide more communicative power than formulaic phrases because they convey specific, meaningful information that helps the speaker get their needs met more effectively.[6]

Moving beyond requesting to include commenting, labeling, and other declarative functions requires specific instructional strategies, such as:

- **High-interest materials.** Using materials with movement, sound, or interactive elements naturally draws attention and creates opportunities for commenting.
- **Milieu teaching methods.** Techniques such as modeling (demonstrating AAC use during activities), mand-modeling (requesting communication), and time delay (providing expectant pauses) can facilitate declarative communication within natural contexts.
- **Motivational content.** Building declarative communication around the learner's interests ensures that commenting and labeling serve meaningful functions rather than appearing as academic exercises.

The organization and presentation of AAC vocabulary significantly impacts user motivation and success. Research suggests several important considerations, including:

- **Response effort.** Systems that require excessive navigation or complex motor patterns may reduce motivation to communicate. Starting with smaller, more manageable displays and gradually increasing complexity can build confidence and competence.
- **Schematic vs. taxonomic organization.** For beginning users, organizing vocabulary by activity or context (all farm-related words together) may be more efficient than taxonomic organization (all animals in one category, all colors in another).[7]
- **Visual scene displays vs. grid displays.** Some learners show preferences for visual scene displays (embedded hotspots in photographs) over traditional grid displays, while others prefer grids. Individual assessment should guide display selection.[8]
- **Consistent motor patterns.** While maintaining consistent symbol locations supports motor learning, starting with smaller displays and gradually expanding may be preferable to overwhelming learners with large grids from the beginning.[9]

Successful AAC implementation requires seamless collaboration among all team members. The device belongs to the client, not to any individual professional, and this principle should guide all team interactions.

Defining Roles and Responsibilities

Clear role definition prevents conflicts and ensures comprehensive support:

- **Speech-language pathologists** typically take the lead on assessment, device programming, and communication goal development while providing training to other team members.

- **Behavior analysts** contribute expertise in motivation, systematic instruction, and data collection while supporting communication skill generalization.
- **Educators** facilitate AAC integration across academic activities and peer interactions while providing classroom-based implementation support.
- **Families** offer crucial insights into communication needs across environments while supporting home-based practice and maintenance.
- **Paraprofessionals and support staff** provide daily implementation support and feedback about system effectiveness in natural environments.

While collaborative input is essential for vocabulary selection and goal setting, having one designated person responsible for device programming often prevents conflicts and ensures consistency. This approach allows for systematic vocabulary organization while incorporating input from all team members.

Regular team meetings should address:

- Progress toward communication goals
- Vocabulary needs and updates
- Technical issues and solutions
- Training needs for team members
- Environmental modifications to support communication

Other areas to think about with intervention are being culturally responsive and linguistically appropriate. This includes:

- Incorporating family communication patterns and preferences
- Respecting cultural values around communication and technology
- Ensuring vocabulary reflects the learner's cultural and linguistic background
- Providing training and support in the family's preferred language

Team members may be hesitant if they are new to AAC. We want to keep the entire team, including the AAC user top of mind! Successful home implementation requires:

- Family training and ongoing support
- Natural integration into daily routines
- Backup plans for device problems
- Clear communication between home and school

Video examples of home AAC use demonstrate the potential for natural integration when families receive adequate support and training.

School implementation involves:

- Staff training across all personnel
- Integration into academic activities
- Peer awareness and support
- Clear policies about device access and care

The concept of "AAC parking" spaces in gymnasiums and playgrounds demonstrates institutional commitment to communication access across all school environments.

Community use requires:

- Portable, durable devices
- Family confidence in public use
- Community awareness and acceptance
- Emergency communication plans

Data collection is always something that I think about when setting goals. It should be individualized but keeping the following items top of mind is important:

- Frequency of spontaneous communication attempts
- Variety of communicative functions
- Message complexity and grammatical development
- Communication across different environments and partners
- User satisfaction and engagement

Progress monitoring should be ongoing and involve all team members in documenting communication growth and system effectiveness.

Goal setting for AAC can be a bit overwhelming if you are new to it! I have included a snippet of some of the goals on our AAC goal bank. The entire goal bank is available in the supplemental section of the book available at www.abaspeech.org. We want to make sure that we include the entire team when goal setting, as communication is important across the learner's day!

If you want some inspiration for getting started using the AAC device in therapy, I hope you will enjoy our go-to AAC activities!

Sample AAC Activities

Playdough Talk
- **Activity:** Make different shapes, animals, or food with playdough.
- **Targets:** Labeling the different shapes made or requesting the therapist to make something specific

Farm Animal Adventure

- **Activity:** Use a toy barn and animals. Have students "help" animals go in/out of the barn.
- **Targets:** Labeling the different animals or requesting animals they want to play with; labeling actions the animals are doing

Bubble Time

- **Activity:** Blowing bubbles
- **Targets:** "Bubbles" "Pop" "More bubbles"

Mystery Bag

- **Activity:** Put objects in a bag. Kids pull one out and name or describe it.
- **Targets:** Based on what smaller objects or mini objects you put in the bag

Feed the Animals

- **Activity:** Grab some small stuffed animals and play food.
- **Targets:** Labeling the food the animals are eating; labeling the animals; requesting the food to feed the animals; requesting the animals to feed; using the action word "eating"

CONCLUSION

AAC implementation represents a complex interplay of assessment, technology, instruction, and collaboration. Success requires moving beyond simplistic approaches to embrace comprehensive, individualized strategies that honor the learner's developmental patterns, preferences, and communication rights.

The transformation witnessed in learners like Timmy, from isolation and frustration to meaningful communication, demonstrates the profound impact of well-implemented AAC. However, this transformation requires sustained commitment from entire teams working together with expertise, patience, and unwavering belief in every individual's potential to communicate.

As we continue to refine our understanding of AAC best practices, we must remember that the goal is not simply to teach device use but to unlock human potential for connection, expression, and participation in the world. Every button press, every spontaneous comment, and every meaningful exchange represents a victory in the fundamental human endeavor of sharing our thoughts and feelings with others.

The field of AAC will continue to evolve, but the core principles remain constant: respect for individual differences, commitment to comprehensive assessment, emphasis on motivation and meaning, and unwavering dedication to collaborative practice. When these principles guide our work, we create opportunities for individuals to find their voice and claim their rightful place as full participants in their communities.

Through careful assessment, thoughtful intervention, and collaborative implementation, AAC can transform lives by providing the tools necessary for authentic human communication. The journey from first button press to complex conversation may be long, but every step represents progress toward the fundamental goal of helping every individual find their unique voice in the world.

NOTES

1. Adapted from the *Assessment of Learning Process (ALP) for Powered Mobility* (Nilsson & Durkin, 2014; Nilsson et al., 2011).

2. Clarke, V., & Tobii Dynavox. (2023). *Dynamic AAC Goals Grid Instructions, Third Edition.* myTobiiDynavox.

3. Semmler, Frick, B. J., Bean, A., & Wagner, L. (2024). Examining core vocabulary with language development for early symbolic communicators. *International Journal of Speech-Language Pathology, 26*(1), 28–37. https://doi.org/10.1080/17549507.2022.2162126

4. Binger, C., Kent-Walsh, J., Harrington, N., & Hollerbach, Q. C. (2020). Tracking Early Sentence-Building Progress in Graphic Symbol Communication. *Language, Speech, and Hearing Services in Schools, 51*(2), 317–328. https://doi.org/10.1044/2019_LSHSS-19-00065

5. Bruinsma, Y., Minjarez, M. B., Schreibman, L., & Stahmer, A. C. (2020). *Naturalistic Developmental Behavioral Interventions for Autism Spectrum Disorder.* Paul H. Brookes Publishing Co.

6. Brown, R. (1973). *A First Language: The Early Stages.* Harvard University Press.

7. Beukelman, David, & Light, Janice (2020). *Augmentative and Alternative Communication: Supporting Children and Adults with Complex Communication Needs*, 5th Edition. Brookes Publishing.

8. Gevarter, C., Horan, K., & Sigafoos, J. (2020). Teaching preschoolers with autism to use different speech-generating device display formats during play: intervention and secondary factors. *Language, Speech, and Hearing Services in Schools, 51*(3), 821–838. https://doi.org/10.1044/2020_LSHSS-19-00092

9. Gevarter, C., Groll, M., & Stone, E. (2020). Dynamic assessment of augmentative and alternative communication application grid formats and communicative targets for children with autism spectrum disorder. *Augmentative and Alternative Communication, 36*(4), 226–237. https://doi.org/10.1080/07434618.2020.1845236

CHAPTER 10

Functional First: Writing IEP Goals That Prepare Students for Real Life

In 2003, I started my position at a school specializing in autism. I was very new to the field, thrilled to be supporting autistic students, but intimidated by goal setting for students who were not yet speaking. I was working with a student who had unsafe behavior, had no way to communicate with the world, and I was just not sure where to start. He really struggled with engaging in any structured activities, so a true assessment was tough.

I knew he was not able to answer yes/no questions to orient his environment, so a goal was set for this. After about three sessions, I realized how very difficult it can be to answer yes/no questions. We ended up amending the IEP because I realized that there were so many other building blocks before getting to this goal. Strengthening joint attention, receptive language skills, and requesting were all more functional for this student. Therefore, the goal of this chapter is to inspire you to effectively create individualized goals that will allow your students to thrive and find their voice.

Developing effective Individualized Education Program (IEP) goals for autistic students represents one of the most critical aspects of our jobs as speech therapists. The process requires a deep understanding of our student's current communication skills, evidence-based assessment practices, and functional goal-setting principles. This chapter provides comprehensive guidance for creating meaningful, measurable, and functional IEP goals that support autistic students across their educational journey.

The importance of well-crafted IEP goals cannot be overstated. These goals serve as the roadmap for a student's educational progress, guiding intervention strategies, measuring outcomes, and ensuring accountability for therapeutic services. Setting the right goals can help guide our students to strengthen their communication skills and overall independence and joy. Setting ineffective goals can cause frustration for the student and practitioner alike.

Assessing autistic students presents unique challenges that directly impact goal development. Traditional standardized assessments may not capture the true abilities of students who struggle with sitting at a table, following unfamiliar directions, or engaging with novel materials. Many autistic students cannot demonstrate their skills in artificial testing environments, making it difficult to establish accurate baselines and appropriate goals.

The assessment process must account for sensory sensitivities, communication differences, and varying levels of social engagement. Students may have significant skills that remain hidden due to assessment methodology limitations. Without robust assessment data, intervention planning becomes guesswork, and IEP goals may miss the mark.

THREE COMPONENTS OF EFFECTIVE ASSESSMENT

Effective assessment for IEP goal development requires three critical components: formal measures, informal measures, and systematic observation. This robust approach provides a comprehensive view of student abilities and needs:

1. **Formal measures** should be selected carefully based on the student's presentation and needs. Refer back to Chapter 1 to learn about more formal measures that may be appropriate for students. The following measures are discussed more in depth. At times, true formal measures may be difficult to administer for autistic students or any student who is not yet speaking. So while these measures are not true formal measures that yield a standardized score, they do give us a good starting point for understanding a student's current communication skills.

   The Functional Communication Profile serves as an excellent tool for students who cannot engage in traditional standardized testing. This assessment evaluates communication across multiple domains and contexts, providing valuable insights into both strengths and areas of need. For preschool-aged students, the *Functional Communication Profile, Preschool Edition* offers developmentally appropriate assessment items.

   The Communication Matrix provides another valuable assessment option, particularly for students with complex communication needs. This free or low-cost online assessment evaluates early communication skills and considers alternative forms of communication. It examines the four primary reasons people communicate and breaks down communication into manageable levels, making it particularly useful for students who are not yet speaking or who use alternative communication methods.

For students receiving Applied Behavior Analysis (ABA) services, the *Verbal Behavior Milestones Assessment and Placement Program (VB-MAPP)* may provide additional insights. This criterion-referenced assessment examines requesting, labeling, social skills, and group participation abilities. Even if speech-language pathologists do not administer the VB-MAPP directly, reviewing existing reports can inform IEP goal development.

2. **Informal measures** complement formal assessments by capturing functional skills in natural environments. Refer to Appendix E Informal Assessments to utilize the informal measures I have developed for members of the ABA Speech Connection.

3. **Systematic observation** in natural environments provides crucial information about how students function in their typical educational settings. Observing students during routine activities, social interactions, and academic tasks reveals information that formal assessments may miss. The informal assessments included in Appendix E will also give a place to document these observations.

For a more detailed overview regarding assessment, refer to Chapter 1.

RAPPORT BUILDING PRIOR TO ASSESSMENT

Before any meaningful assessment can occur, establishing rapport with students is essential. This process requires patience, flexibility, and understanding. Evaluators should avoid demanding communication, use simple language, and strive to be playful when appropriate.

I always try to live by the motto, "Be a giver not a taker," a concept I was first introduced to by my friend and colleague, Tamara Kasper. I had the opportunity to see Tamara present an all-day workshop in 2010 in Houston, Texas. She discussed working with emergent communicators in a way that I loved! Tamara shared real-life experiences and strategies that I could start incorporating into my work. Rather than removing preferred items or interrupting preferred activities within our assessment or therapy, we should instead introduce new, engaging materials and activities. We should try to not take away items from our students—they might have difficulty protesting. We need to keep that top of mind throughout our work. This approach reduces anxiety and increases the likelihood of observing authentic student communication.

FRAMEWORK FOR FUNCTIONAL GOAL DEVELOPMENT

The SMART goal framework, developed by George Doran in 1981, provides essential structure for IEP goal development. SMART stands for Specific, Measurable, Attainable, Results-oriented (or Relevant), and Time-bound. Each component plays a crucial role in creating goals that drive meaningful progress.[1]

Specific

Identify the skill or behavior being targeted. Vague language leads to confusion about expectations and difficulty measuring progress. Instead of writing, "Student will improve communication," a specific goal states, "Student will request preferred items using single words."

Measurable

Goals must specify how progress will be measured, whether through accuracy percentages, duration, frequency, or other quantifiable measures. The measurement system should be practical for implementation while providing meaningful data.

Attainable

Apply realistic expectations based on current student abilities and individual characteristics. Goals should represent meaningful progress without being so ambitious that they set students up for failure. For example, a student who struggles to engage in therapy and is not yet speaking, should not have a goal to engage in a three-step peer conversation.

Results-oriented or Relevant

Focus on meaningful outcomes that impact student functioning. Goals should address skills that enhance independence, communication, or quality of life. The relevance of each goal should be clear to all team members. This will be an individualized part of the goal development process. It can be difficult at times to get all team members on the same page about the relevance of goals; just remember: We all want what is best for our students!

Time-bound

Include specific time frames for achievement, typically within the annual IEP period. This component ensures accountability and provides structure for progress monitoring.

Including baseline data in IEP goals is vital for demonstrating need and measuring progress. *Baseline data* represents student performance without intervention or support. This information should appear in the present levels of performance section and directly connect to proposed goals.

Baseline data serves multiple purposes. It justifies the need for specialized services, provides a starting point for measuring progress, and helps teams make data-based decisions about intervention effectiveness. Without clear baseline data, teams cannot determine whether interventions are working or when goals have been achieved.

For example, if a student needs to learn to label functional items, the baseline might state: "When presented with 10 common objects, Sarah can independently label 2 items (20% accuracy) without prompting." This specific baseline allows for clear measurement of progress throughout the IEP year.

GOALS, OBJECTIVES, AND NAVIGATING STATE STANDARDS

The relationship between goals and objectives is like a journey. The overall annual IEP goal represents the destination. Objectives represent the individual steps needed to reach that destination.

Annual IEP goals describe the overarching skill or behavior the student should achieve by the end of the IEP year. These goals are broad enough to encompass the general skill area while remaining specific enough to be measurable.

Objectives break the larger annual goal into different, smaller skill sets that build toward the larger goal. Objectives represent prerequisite skills or component skills necessary for achieving the annual goal. For example, suppose the annual goal involves answering six personal safety questions. In that case, objectives might include the ability to answer two personal safety goals by a certain date and other objectives would be building more questions until the goal has been reached.

Federal law requires objectives for students taking alternate assessments, but states and districts have flexibility in determining requirements for other students. Some states mandate objectives for all IEP goals, while others leave the decision to local districts. Understanding local requirements prevents compliance issues while ensuring appropriate goal structure.

The variation in requirements across states and districts highlights the importance of understanding local policies. What works in one location may not meet requirements in another. IEP team members should clarify expectations before goal development begins.

Many states require IEP goals to align with state academic standards, while others use common core standards or alternative frameworks. For students significantly below grade level, this requirement can create challenges in goal development.

When students perform multiple grade levels below their chronological peers, teams must identify appropriate prerequisite skills that align with academic standards. This process requires understanding both the vertical progression of skills within domains and the individual student's current abilities.

Extended or alternative standards provide options for students with significant cognitive disabilities. These standards maintain alignment with general education content while providing developmentally appropriate expectations. Speech-language pathologists and special educators should familiarize themselves with available alternative standards in their states.

For students working significantly below grade level, creating a bridge between current abilities and grade-level expectations requires careful planning. Teams must identify the prerequisite skills students need to work toward grade-level standards, even if achieving those standards within one IEP year is unrealistic.

This process involves analyzing task demands, identifying component skills, and sequencing instruction to build toward more complex abilities. Matrix training approaches can help students generalize skills more efficiently by teaching a subset of examples that promote broader skill acquisition.

So, knowing where to start can be a challenge. I like to include foundational skills into my IEP planning for students who are not yet speaking or who are emergent communicators. For preschool and early elementary students, eight foundational skills form the basis for more advanced communication and academic learning. These skills create the scaffolding necessary for future educational success.

FOUNDATIONAL SKILLS FOR STUDENT SUCCESS

Elementary

1. **Joint attention** represents one of the most critical foundational skills. Joint attention involves shared focus between two or more people on an object or event, with all parties aware of the shared focus. Research demonstrates strong relationships between joint attention abilities and later language development.

   Joint attention goals might target engaging in shared activities with adults for specified durations. Implementation can occur through book reading, where student and therapist look at pictures together; song activities with visual supports; or toy play with turn-taking elements. The key is creating genuine moments of shared engagement rather than forced interaction. This is discussed in Chapter 3 with the Connect and Engage Method.

   Here are a few goals from my Autism IEP Goal Bank:
   a. Student will engage in a shared *literacy-based* activity for a duration of three minutes, without prompts, over three consecutive sessions.
   b. Student will engage in a shared *movement-based* activity for a duration of three minutes, without prompts, over three consecutive sessions.
   c. Student will engage in a shared *play-based* activity for a duration of three minutes, without prompts, over three consecutive sessions.
   d. Student will engage in a shared *music-based* activity for a duration of three minutes, without prompts, over three consecutive sessions.

2. **Imitation skills** provide the foundation for learning through observation. Both motor and verbal imitation contribute to overall communication development. Motor imitation goals might target copying gross motor movements or play-based activities. Modified Simon Says games provide engaging ways to work on motor imitation while maintaining student interest.

Verbal imitation becomes particularly important for students who are beginning to develop speech. For younger students, verbal imitation may emerge naturally during play activities. Older students may benefit from more structured verbal imitation activities using picture cards or specific sound sequences.

Examples:

a. The student will imitate gross motor movements, when shown a movement by the instructor, without prompts, over three consecutive sessions.

b. The student will imitate actions taking place during a play-based activity when shown an action by the instructor, without prompts, over three consecutive sessions.

c. Given a therapist model, the student will imitate functional one-syllable words, with 90% accuracy, over three consecutive sessions.

d. Given a therapist model, the student will imitate functional two-syllable words, with 90% accuracy, over three consecutive sessions.

3. **Requesting or manding** skills allow students to communicate their wants and needs effectively. These skills often provide the most immediate functional benefit for students and families. Requesting goals should target both items and actions, allowing students to communicate across various contexts. Direct instruction on requesting shows a student that their communication is powerful. Students learn: "I do something, I get something." It is transformative to see a learner understand that their communication has power!

Example:

a. Student will request specific items or actions (a total of five) during a 25-minute structured activity, without prompts, over three consecutive sessions.

Effective requesting instruction often uses natural opportunities throughout the day. Direct instruction should embed requesting opportunities into preferred activities and routines. Sensory bins, art activities, and play scenarios provide rich opportunities for requesting practice.

4. **Matching skills** support cognitive development and vocabulary expansion. Students can work on matching identical objects, identical pictures, or objects to pictures. These skills contribute to categorization abilities, visual discrimination, and attention to detail.

Matching activities should incorporate preferred items and themes when possible. Using characters from favorite books or movies increases student engagement and motivation. The complexity of matching tasks can gradually increase as students demonstrate mastery.

Example:

a. When presented with a field of three pictures and given a picture and the direction "Match (targeted item)," the student will match to the correct category without prompts, over three consecutive sessions.

5. **Labeling skills** help students develop expressive vocabulary for communication. However, labeling goals should first focus on preferred and functional items rather than arbitrary vocabulary targets. Students should work on labeling items they genuinely care about first, this makes the task more fun and motivating for our students.

   The selection of labeling targets requires careful consideration. Items that students find aversive or difficult to use may not be appropriate early labeling targets. Instead, focusing on preferred foods, favorite characters, or enjoyable activities increases the likelihood of success and maintains motivation. We would not want to work on labeling "bathroom" if the student is on a toileting program and finds the bathroom aversive. We would want to work on labeling *Daniel the Tiger* if that was a favorite show of our students. Refer back to Figure 5.1 Teaching Labels Strategically for a quick reference.

   This is also a good time to remember our discussion about using multiple examples. If we are working on labeling *Daniel the Tiger*, we want to use three picture examples. This helps us plan for the generalization of language skills and is an important part of the intervention process!

   a. Student will label preferred items when shown a picture with 90% accuracy, over three consecutive sessions.

   b. Student will label functional items when shown a picture, with 90% accuracy, over three consecutive sessions.

   c. Student will label actions when shown a picture or the actual action, with 90% accuracy, over three consecutive sessions.

6. **Phrase construction** builds on labeling using single words and by combining words into meaningful phrases. Early phrase construction often follows predictable patterns such as "action + object" (eating apple) or "attribute + object" (big ball). Matrix training approaches can help students generate novel phrases without teaching every possible combination. We discuss this more complex topic in a CEU course in the ABA Speech Connection about Matrix Training.

   Examples:

   a. When presented with a picture of an action taking place, the student will create a two-word phrase to describe the picture with 90% accuracy, over three consecutive sessions.

   b. When presented with a picture of an action taking place, the student will create a grammatically correct sentence to describe the picture with 90% accuracy, over three consecutive sessions.

7. **Fill-in-the-blank activities** provide structured opportunities for verbal participation and early social reciprocity. These activities support social engagement and provide stepping stones toward more advanced conversation skills.

Common fill-in-the-blank activities include familiar songs ("Old MacDonald Had a ___"), repetitive book reading (*Brown Bear, Brown Bear, What Do You ___*), and routine activities ("Ready, set, ___"). These activities create predictable opportunities for successful communication while building turn-taking skills.

Example:

a. When given a fill in the blank phrase, Joe will use a logical word to fill in the blank (a total of 15 phrases) without prompts, over three consecutive sessions.

Secondary

As students transition through elementary into secondary education, IEP goals must shift toward preparing them for adult independence and employment. The foundational skills developed in earlier years should evolve into practical abilities that support community participation and vocational success.

The ultimate objectives for older students include independent communication, enjoyable leisure activities, competitive employment opportunities, and overall life satisfaction. These outcomes require careful goal planning that considers both immediate educational needs and long-term life goals:

1. **Following directions for vocational tasks** represents a critical skill area for older students. Goals might target following multistep directions to gather needed materials, complete workplace tasks, or organize workspaces. Task analysis approaches can break complex job requirements into teachable components.

    For example, a student working in a school office might need to follow directions to sort mail, make copies, or organize supplies. Each task requires understanding specific vocabulary, following sequential steps, and completing work to acceptable standards.

    Example:

    a. The student will follow all items on a task analysis of a vocational task (making copies, doing recycling, etc...) with no more than one prompt, over three consecutive sessions.

2. **Functional expressive language** goals focus on vocabulary and communication skills directly related to vocational and community activities. Students need to label work materials, describe completed tasks, and communicate about their work experiences.

    Rather than working on arbitrary vocabulary lists, older students should focus on words and phrases they will use in actual work environments. This might include equipment names, action words related to job tasks, or social communication phrases needed for workplace interaction.

Examples:

a. The student will label vocational items without prompts, over three consecutive sessions without prompts.
b. The student will label vocational actions without prompts, over three consecutive sessions without prompts.
c. When presented with a functional vocabulary term, the student will label the item, describe the function, and provide two other details about the item, without prompts, over three consecutive sessions.

3. **Task completion and reporting** skills allow students to work independently and communicate about their progress. Goals might target completing assigned tasks within specified time frames and reporting completion to supervisors or teachers.

   These skills require understanding task expectations, managing time effectively, and communicating appropriately with authority figures. Students need explicit instruction in how to ask for help, report problems, and indicate when work is finished.

   Example:

a. After completing a vocational task, students will independently tell a supervisor that they have completed the task independently over three consecutive days.

4. **Cooperative leisure activities** provide opportunities for social interaction while building skills that can transfer to community and home settings. Modified games and activities allow students to practice turn-taking, following rules, and engaging with peers in structured environments.

   Modified Uno represents an excellent cooperative leisure activity that can be adapted for various skill levels. The game requires turn-taking, rule following, and social interaction while remaining enjoyable and motivating. Video models can teach game rules and social expectations before students practice with peers.

   The grocery store game provides another engaging group activity that builds cooperation and social skills. Students take turns naming items beginning with sequential letters of the alphabet, creating a collaborative story about a shopping trip. Visual supports can assist students who need additional prompting.

   Examples:

- Student will participate in a small group activity for 15 minutes and attend to the teacher, without prompts, over three consecutive sessions.
- Student will respond to four different group instructions without prompts, over three consecutive sessions.

5. **Independent leisure skills** help students develop activities they can enjoy throughout their lives. Yoga instruction provides physical activity, stress reduction, and a skill that transfers to community fitness programs. Students can learn basic poses and sequences that promote physical health and emotional regulation.

Water bottle weightlifting offers another accessible leisure activity that requires minimal equipment and can be adapted for various ability levels. Students can follow exercise routines, count repetitions, and track their progress over time.

Example:

Student will engage in an independent leisure activity (a total of four) for a duration of 10 minutes with no more than one prompt, over three consecutive sessions.

6. **Community participation skills** prepare students for independent functioning in community settings. Goals might address navigating community locations, using public transportation, or engaging with community services.

   For students who will continue living with family support, goals might focus on contributing to household responsibilities, engaging in community recreation programs, or accessing services independently.

   Example:

   Student will use credit/debit cards to make purchases, completing 80% of task-analysis steps independently, in four to five consecutive opportunities.

7. **Self-advocacy skills** become increasingly important as students approach transition age. Students need to communicate their needs, preferences, and concerns to various adults in their lives. Goals might target asking for help when needed, expressing preferences about activities, or communicating about accommodations.

   The IEP meeting represents the culmination of assessment and goal development efforts. Creating positive meeting experiences requires proactive planning and collaborative approaches that respect all team members' perspectives and expertise.

   Example:

   Student will request break, reduced demand or some environmental adjustment when presented with known nonpreferred conditions with or without prompts in four to five opportunities for 9 to 10 consecutive school days.

AAC is another area that can be beneficial for students who are emerging communicators. Knowing how to goal-set for this area just like all areas will be based on an assessment. Some goal areas that may be beneficial for your student are device operation and navigation, getting started with communication, requesting, labeling, vocabulary, descriptive language, social skills, comprehension, group participation, academics, self-advocacy, retelling, and device use and care. Below are three AAC goal examples:

1. The student will independently turn on their AAC device and navigate to the home screen within 30 seconds, over three consecutive sessions.
2. The student will use their AAC device to label common objects (minimum of 10) when shown objects or pictures, with 90% accuracy over three consecutive sessions.
3. The student will use their AAC device to share information about personal experiences or interests during conversations, at least twice per conversation, over three consecutive sessions.

Developing effective IEP goals requires comprehensive assessment, collaborative team processes, and careful attention to individual student needs and characteristics. The process begins with robust assessment that captures student abilities across multiple contexts and continues through collaborative goal development that considers both immediate needs and long-term outcomes.

The foundational skills approach for younger students creates the building blocks necessary for future learning and communication development. As students progress through their educational careers, goals should evolve to address independence, vocational preparation, and community participation skills.

Successful IEP development requires proactive planning, clear communication, and ongoing collaboration among all team members. When teams work together effectively and focus on functional, meaningful goals, students can make significant progress.

The investment in quality IEP development pays dividends throughout a student's educational career and beyond. Well-crafted goals provide direction for instruction, criteria for measuring progress, and accountability for educational services. Most importantly, effective IEP goals help students develop the skills they need to communicate, learn, and participate fully in their communities.

Through careful attention to assessment, goal development, and team collaboration, educational professionals can create IEP goals that truly serve the needs of students with autism and support their journey toward independence and success.

View the Autism IEP Goal Bank in Appendix F.

NOTE

1. Doran, George T. (1981). There's a S.M.A.R.T. way to write management's goals and objectives. *Management Review, 70*(11): 35–36.

CHAPTER 11

IEP Meeting Mastery: From Data Presentation to Goal Approval in 60 Minutes

Sometimes IEP meetings can be very rewarding, like the time a parent cried tears of joy because their child was talking, and a previous teacher had said that would never happen. Not all IEP meetings go smoothly. When a transfer student arrived, we quickly developed a new IEP based on updated information and sent the draft home a week early with no feedback from the family. Since our first meeting went well, we didn't invite the special education director, but the family arrived with an advocate known for being difficult.

In this chapter I'll share strategies to prepare for IEP meetings and we will finish with three communication strategies. I want you to feel confident every time you walk into an IEP.

This chapter explores the multifaceted aspects of IEP meetings, from preparation strategies to communication techniques, grounded in both ethical guidelines and research-based practices. Whether you are a seasoned professional or new to the IEP process, understanding how to approach these meetings with confidence and competence is essential to serving students with disabilities effectively.

WHAT WE SAID WE WOULD DO

The IEP serves as a cornerstone document in special education, mandated by the Individuals with Disabilities Education Act (IDEA). This legislation ensures that students with disabilities have access to a free and appropriate public education designed to prepare them for future education, independent living, and employment. The IEP functions as both a planning tool and a legal document, outlining the student's current abilities, educational goals, evaluation criteria, and the specific services the student will receive.

Unlike general education lesson plans that teachers can modify at will, the IEP represents a binding commitment from the school district. Every service minute, every accommodation, and every goal must be implemented as written unless the team reconvenes to make changes. This legal weight underscores why IEP meetings require such careful attention and why many professionals approach them with a mixture of purpose and trepidation.

I remember attending an ethics session at the ASHA Schools Conference in Baltimore in 2023. The speaker said, "The IEP is what we said we would do." That line always stuck with me. It is brief but to the point.

The American Speech-Language-Hearing Association (ASHA) Code of Ethics provides clear guidance for speech-language pathologists participating in IEP meetings. Recently updated, these ethical principles emphasize three key responsibilities relevant to the IEP process:

1. **Resourceful communication.** Professionals must use every available resource, including referral and professional collaboration when appropriate, to ensure quality service provision. In the context of IEP meetings, this means reaching out to all relevant stakeholders, including private therapists, medical professionals, and community providers to gather comprehensive information about the student. A speech-language pathologist (SLP) working with a student who also receives private therapy should make every effort to communicate with that provider, ensuring goals complement rather than conflict with one another.

2. **Continuing education.** The code emphasizes lifelong learning and continuous professional development. The field of communication disorders evolves constantly, with new research informing best practices for assessment and intervention. Professionals who commit to ongoing education, whether through formal coursework, professional conferences, or structured learning communities, position themselves to provide more effective services and feel more confident in their expertise during IEP meetings.

3. **Professionalism.** Professionals must avoid conduct that adversely reflects on the profession or their fitness to serve. During contentious IEP meetings, when emotions run high and disagreements emerge, maintaining professional composure becomes paramount. While professionals should never tolerate verbal abuse, they must strive to remain calm, respectful, and focused on the student's needs even in challenging circumstances. When I was in graduate school, I never imagined that I would be in IEP meetings in which I discussed one goal for one hour or meetings where I saw other team members leave crying, but I have. We will discuss how to prepare all types of IEP meetings.

SIX STRATEGIES FOR IEP MEETINGS

Strategy 1: Collaboration

Effective IEP meetings begin long before team members gather around the conference table. Collaboration with all stakeholders should occur throughout the year, not just in the weeks leading up to the annual review. This is easier said than done! Time is a big commodity, especially when you work in the schools, but trying to carve out time for ongoing communication with other providers and parents will make the IEP feel less stressful.

For school-based professionals, this means establishing communication systems with parents that extend beyond required progress reports. Regular informal updates, whether through email, a shared Google doc, or brief phone calls build relationships and keep families informed about their child's progress. When annual IEP meetings arrive, parents who have received consistent communication throughout the year feel more connected to the process and better prepared to participate meaningfully.

At the start of a new school year, I would email each parent on my caseload. This took a lot of time, but it was a solid way to get our relationship off on the right foot. My email template was as follows:

Hi (   ). My name is Rose Griffin. I just wanted to write and let you know that I will be (Child's name) speech therapist at (school name). I look forward to supporting their communication goals this year. If you have any questions or just want to reach out and say hi, please reply to this email.

Best, Rose Griffin

Sending an email to each parent takes a lot of time at the start of the school year, but it was always a good way to start the therapeutic relationship.

Collaboration with related service providers requires similar intentionality. A student receiving both school-based and private speech therapy benefits when both therapists coordinate their approaches. This might involve quarterly phone calls to discuss progress, share strategies, and ensure therapeutic goals complement one another. School districts require parent permission for such communication; securing this authorization early in the school year facilitates ongoing collaboration. Usually at a minimum, I would get signed permission at the start of the school year. I would reach out to the outside therapist at the beginning of the school year to discuss the student and their current progress, I would reach out again before the IEP meeting to get the most recent information regarding progress.

Collaboration with special education and general education teachers proves equally important, particularly for students who spend significant time in inclusive settings. Special education professionals should meet with teachers before IEP meetings to discuss how the student functions in the classroom setting, what supports the teacher needs, and how IEP goals can support success in that setting. These conversations give us a better understanding of how the student is communicating in the larger school environment.

After we have discussed how a student is doing across their day, we will want to make sure that we have current data about how the student is doing with specific goals and skills. This data will allow us to demonstrate a need for any goals that we may set.

Strategy 2: Data Collection

Baseline data provides the foundation for meaningful IEP goals. It answers the question: "What skills does the student have before intervention?" Without clear information about a student's initial performance level, teams cannot establish appropriate targets or measure progress effectively.

Including baseline data serves multiple purposes. First, it demonstrates a need for intervention or continued service. When teams can show that a student currently performs a skill at 20% accuracy, the rationale for targeting that skill becomes evident. Second, baseline data provides a starting point for measuring progress. Teams can track improvement from the baseline through instruction and intervention, documenting the student's learning trajectory. Third, specific baseline data focuses discussions on appropriate goal targets rather than debates about student abilities.

Effective baseline data should be *recent*, *relevant*, and *comprehensive*. Recent data is ideally collected within the month preceding the IEP meeting and provides current information about student abilities. Older data may no longer accurately represent the student's skills, particularly for young children or students making rapid progress. Relevant data connects directly to the skills being targeted in IEP goals. If you want to gather baseline data on a specific skill like labeling actions, you may use, for example, three to five actions. Show the student the pictures of the actions or the actions in real life and chart the percentage of actions they can label correctly.

When presenting baseline data in IEP meetings, professionals should strive for clarity and accessibility. Rather than overwhelming parents with data sheets or technical graphs, synthesize information into understandable statements:

Over the past two weeks, we collected data during five different therapy sessions. Marcus was able to label common objects correctly about 3 out of 10 times, or 30% accuracy. This shows us he's beginning to learn these words but needs continued support to use them more consistently.

Once we have baseline data, we can now clearly set our goals. Goal clarity directly impacts implementation effectiveness. Vague or poorly written goals create confusion about expectations, make data collection difficult, and complicate progress monitoring. Every IEP goal should answer several key questions:

1. What exactly will the student do?
2. How well must they do it? Under what conditions?
3. How will we know when the goal is met?

Goal writing is something I got better at and felt more confident with over the years. It doesn't happen overnight, so be patient. I was cleaning the storage part to our basement last year and I came across my lesson plans and paperwork from my Clinical Fellowship Year (CFY). I cringed reading them! Why did I write goals for answering yes/no questions for students who were emerging communicators? Why did I write goals to work on direct eye contact in a way that was not naturalistic? When we know better, we do better. Don't be hard on yourself. This is a skill that you will strengthen with each IEP (and hopefully after reading this book and using our resources!). Just know that if you get stuck, you can contact me; I am here to be a support.

Strategy 3: Clear Goal Writing

Strategy three is clear goal writing. Remember, effective goals are SMART (Specific, Measurable, Attainable, Relevant, Timely). Consider this goal: "Henry will increase his overall expressive language skills by labeling functional items a total of 12 with 90% accuracy over three consecutive sessions." This goal specifies the exact behavior (labeling functional items), quantifies the target (12 items), establishes the performance criterion (90% accuracy), and defines the mastery requirement (two consecutive sessions). A teacher or therapist reading this goal understands precisely what to teach, how to collect data, and when to consider the goal mastered.

The number of targets (in this case, 12 items) should reflect the individual student's learning profile and needs. For a student just beginning to develop expressive vocabulary, mastering 12 new labels might represent significant, meaningful progress. For a student with more advanced language skills, 12 items might be insufficient to demonstrate meaningful growth. The key is individualization based on comprehensive assessment and team discussion about what constitutes meaningful progress for this particular student. This can be very difficult to hypothesize for students who are new to you, but by including a number, we can better demonstrate the progress and growth our learner is making.

Goals should also consider the student's learning environment and daily routines. Functional vocabulary items might include objects and activities the student encounters throughout their day cup, snack, iPad, playground, and bathroom. Selecting targets that connect to the student's real-world experiences increases motivation and provides natural opportunities for practice and reinforcement.

Strategy 4: Sending Home an IEP Draft

Once we have our draft complete, we should send it home to the family. Sending draft IEPs to families in advance represents one of the most effective strategies for promoting positive, collaborative meetings. This practice demonstrates respect for parents' time and input while reducing the likelihood of surprises during meetings.

Draft IEPs should typically be shared one week before the scheduled meeting, allowing families adequate time to review the document, consult with outside providers or advocates if desired, and formulate questions or concerns. The draft should include present levels of performance, proposed goals, and preliminary thoughts about services, while clearly indicating that all elements remain open for discussion and modification. Check with your district to determine if they have a different timeline, some districts are very specific on when things need to be sent, and others are not.

When sending draft IEPs, accompanying communication should emphasize the collaborative nature of the process: For example:

Attached is a draft of Marcus's IEP for your review. Please know that everything in this draft is open for discussion at our meeting. We value your input and want to make sure the final IEP reflects your priorities for Marcus's learning. If you have questions or would like to discuss anything before the meeting, please don't hesitate to reach out.

Some professionals worry that sending draft IEPs suggests predetermination, that the team has already decided what services the student will receive without parent input. However, clearly communicating that the draft serves as a starting point for conversation, not a final decision, addresses this concern. Additionally, incorporating parent feedback received before the meeting demonstrates genuine openness to collaboration.

Districts vary in their policies about draft IEPs. Some require teams to send drafts, recognizing the benefits for family engagement. Others discourage or prohibit the practice, concerned about legal implications. Professionals should understand their district's expectations while advocating for practices that promote family partnership.

If I am the case manager, I send the draft home a week before. I email the parent using the template from above. I also check in with the parents two days before the meeting to check in and answer any questions they may have. I try to do my best when we all sit down for the meeting or we all log onto the meeting that we have shared and been there to incorporate any feedback or answer any questions that they may have.

Strategy 5: Know the Guest List

Understanding who will attend an IEP meeting allows the school team to prepare appropriately and ensure adequate representation. When parents bring advocates, educational consultants, or attorneys to meetings, the school team should include personnel with comparable expertise—typically the special education director or someone well-versed in special education law and district procedures. If parents bring a lawyer, my experience is that the district also needs to have its lawyer present.

Surprises at IEP meetings create stress and can derail productive conversations. When a parent arrives with an unexpected guest, school team members may feel caught off-guard and defensive. Similarly, when school personnel bring unexpected administrators or consultants without informing families, parents may feel ambushed or intimidated.

Advance communication about meeting attendees benefits all parties. Meeting invitations should clearly list who from the school will attend, and families should be asked to inform the school if they plan to bring additional participants. This transparency allows everyone to prepare appropriately and sets the stage for respectful, balanced conversations.

Strategy 6: Get Comfortable with the Content

Confidence in IEP meetings stems largely from thorough preparation and deep knowledge of the student and information included in the document. Professionals who have collected robust assessment data, consulted with relevant stakeholders, written clear goals grounded in that data, and rehearsed their presentation typically feel more confident than those who have prepared at the last minute.

Preparation might involve different strategies for different people. Some professionals benefit from writing out exactly what they plan to say, particularly for complex or potentially contentious points. Others prefer bullet-point notes highlighting key information they want to convey. Still others find that simply reviewing the IEP document several times and mentally rehearsing their presentation provides adequate preparation.

Having visual supports available can increase confidence and clarity. This might mean bringing a printed copy of the IEP to reference during the meeting, preparing a simple handout for parents that summarizes key points in accessible language, or having data graphs or work samples available to illustrate student progress.

Managing premeeting anxiety represents another aspect of feeling comfortable. While some anxiety before important meetings is normal and even adaptive, excessive anxiety can interfere with clear thinking and effective communication. Professionals might develop personal strategies for managing meeting-related stress, whether through physical activity, breathing exercises, positive self-talk, or consultation with supportive colleagues.

Research on effective public speaking provides valuable insights applicable to IEP meeting participation. While some professionals balk at thinking of IEP meetings as "public speaking," these gatherings do require presenting information to a group, often including people in positions of authority and under circumstances that may feel evaluative or high-stakes.

A study examining recommendations from expert speakers identified several key strategies: thorough preparation, use of visual supports, practice, anxiety management, effective delivery, and reflective evaluation. Each element applies directly to IEP meeting participation.

1. **Preparation**, as discussed extensively in this chapter, forms the foundation for confident communication. Professionals who understand their content deeply, anticipate potential questions, and think through how to explain complex concepts in accessible language position themselves for successful meetings.

2. **Visual supports** enhance understanding and retention. In IEP meetings, this might involve graphs showing student progress over time, work samples demonstrating current skills, or simple handouts summarizing proposed goals. Visual information complements verbal explanations, particularly for stakeholders who may be less familiar with educational or clinical terminology.

3. **Practice** allows professionals to refine their message and delivery. This might involve rehearsing alone, presenting to a colleague for feedback, or simply mentally walking through the presentation multiple times. While extensive practice may not be necessary for routine annual reviews, it becomes increasingly valuable for initial evaluations, eligibility meetings, or situations where conflict is anticipated.

4. **Anxiety management** acknowledges that even experienced professionals may feel nervous in certain meeting contexts. Strategies that help manage this anxiety, whether physical (deep breathing, progressive muscle relaxation), cognitive (reframing nervous thoughts, focusing on the student rather than self-evaluation), or social (arriving early to engage in informal conversation, sitting next to a supportive colleague) allow professionals to present information more effectively.

5. **Effective delivery** includes clear articulation, appropriate pacing, and nonverbal communication that conveys confidence and openness. Making eye contact with various team members, using a conversational yet professional tone, and monitoring the group's understanding through verbal and nonverbal feedback all contribute to successful communication.

6. **Reflective evaluation** after meetings allows professionals to identify what went well and what might be improved for future meetings. This might involve informal self-reflection, debriefing with colleagues, or more structured evaluation using a rubric or checklist. Over time, this reflection builds a repertoire of effective strategies and increases confidence in challenging situations.

NAVIGATING CONTENTIOUS MEETINGS

Despite best efforts at preparation and collaboration, some IEP meetings become contentious. Parents may arrive angry about perceived failures in their child's education. Advocates may aggressively question every proposed goal or service. Team members may disagree about appropriate placement or intervention approaches. In these situations, several principles can help maintain productive conversations:

1. **Focus on the student.** When discussions become heated, explicitly redirecting attention to the student's needs can lower tension: "I understand we have different perspectives on this, but I think we all share the goal of helping Sarah communicate more effectively. Let's talk about what approaches might work best for her."

2. **Acknowledge emotions** without becoming defensive. Parents who express frustration or anger often do so from a place of deep concern for their child and previous negative experiences. Responding with empathy, "I can hear how concerned you are about this. Tell me more about what you're seeing at home," validates their feelings without requiring agreement with their position.

3. **Focus on data** rather than opinions. When disagreements arise about student abilities or need refer to objective assessment data: "The assessment results show that Marcus can currently identify 15 letters. Let's look at this data together and talk about what target would represent meaningful progress for him."

4. **Be willing to take breaks** or continue meetings at another time. IEP meetings that stretch for hours with rising tension rarely produce good outcomes. When speech therapists are asked to be a part of lengthy meetings, they need to discuss this with their special education directors, principals, and union representatives when possible. Speech therapists may be missing other students' IEP time during these meetings. Therefore, this will need to be addressed so that the SLP does not feel undue stress when having to attend meetings that are longer than normal.

5. **Know when to involve additional support.** Special education directors, principals, or district personnel with mediation training can sometimes help navigate impasses that the immediate team cannot resolve. While involving additional administrators should not be the first response to every disagreement, it represents an appropriate step when meetings become unproductive despite the team's best efforts.

IEP meetings represent complex professional endeavors requiring careful preparation, ethical practice, collaborative communication, and student-centered decision-making. While the process can feel daunting, particularly for new professionals or in contentious situations, systematic preparation and adherence to ethical guidelines position professionals to navigate these meetings with confidence.

The strategies outlined in this chapter—extensive collaboration, baseline data collection, clear goal writing, advance sharing of draft IEPs, knowing meeting attendees, and thorough content preparation—create conditions for productive meetings. Grounding communication in research-based principles and maintaining focus on the student's needs and best interests helps teams work through disagreements and develop truly individualized programs.

Ultimately, IEP meetings serve one primary purpose: ensuring that students with disabilities receive the education and services they need to reach their potential. When professionals approach these meetings as opportunities for collaboration rather than compliance exercises, when they truly listen to parent perspectives while contributing their expertise, and when they remain steadfastly focused on what will best serve each individual student, IEP meetings become powerful tools for positive change in students' lives.

The investment in quality IEP development, the hours spent collecting data, writing thoughtful goals, collaborating with colleagues, and preparing for meetings pays dividends throughout a student's educational career. Well-crafted IEPs provide clear direction for instruction, meaningful criteria for measuring progress, and accountability for educational services. Most importantly, they help students develop the necessary skills to communicate, learn, and participate fully in their communities, now and into the future.

CHAPTER 12

Ethical Collaboration in Practice

I worked at the Cleveland Clinic Center for Autism, now the Lerner School, and this was where I first learned about the science of applied behavior analysis. I worked with many students, but there was one I will never forget. He was 18 and the kind of student who knew exactly what he wanted in the world but had absolutely no way to communicate. Instead he used unsafe behavior to navigate his environment.

I remember studying his paperwork before our first session and reading all the therapy notes. I asked my friend and co-worker Jamie, "How can this be? What did he do in all those sessions? How could they not reach him?" He had been receiving therapy since the age of two. So, 16 years of special education and he still could not communicate with the world.

I was a speech therapist at the time, but I really enjoyed learning about ABA and collaborating with board certified behavior analysts (BCBAs). I went over the paperwork for my new student with the treating BCBA and we discussed requesting as one of the first skills to address in therapy. Requesting would allow the student to understand that their communication was powerful.

I observed the student, and the next day it was time for our first therapy session. We started the session by requesting music. He loved country music and so did I, so this was fun! We listened to music and then I used a gestural prompt to show him where the country music button was on his AAC device. The device was new for him, and I was nervous that we would be overwhelmed. We listened to Garth Brooks, Shania Twain, and others. And on the third trial he pressed the country music button on his device independently! Amazing!

On one hand it filled me with joy that he was able to communicate on his own for the first time, but on the other hand it broke my heart that it took so long. And in that moment and in so many others that followed, I saw the power of ABA literally transform his life before my eyes, and I was hooked.

THE CALL TO COLLABORATE

As a speech-language pathologist (SLP), you may find yourself working alongside board certified behavior analysts (BCBAs) and registered behavior technicians (RBTs) more frequently than ever before. While this interdisciplinary collaboration holds tremendous promise for the students and clients we serve, it can also present unique challenges. Different training backgrounds, professional vocabularies, and intervention approaches can lead to misunderstandings, conflicts, and missed opportunities for collaboration.

This chapter is designed specifically for SLPs who want to enhance their collaborative relationships with behavior analysts and RBTs. Whether you work in schools, clinics, early intervention programs, or private practice settings, understanding the ethical foundations, training requirements, and communication strategies that facilitate effective collaboration will help you provide the highest quality services to your clients.

Throughout this chapter, we will explore the ethical codes that call us to collaborate, examine the educational backgrounds that shape each profession's perspective, and provide practical strategies for building strong interdisciplinary partnerships. By the end, you will have concrete tools to transform potential conflicts into opportunities for professional growth and, most importantly, improved outcomes for the individuals we serve.

Both American Speech-Language-Hearing Association (ASHA) and the Behavior Analyst Certification Board (BACB) explicitly outline the expectation for interprofessional collaboration in their respective ethical codes. Understanding these ethical foundations is crucial for SLPs because it provides the professional justification for collaborative practices and helps navigate situations where collaboration may be challenging.

The American Speech-Language-Hearing Association's Code of Ethics clearly states that professionals shall work collaboratively when appropriate with members of one's own profession and other professions to deliver the highest quality of care.[1] This principle recognizes that no single professional possesses all the expertise needed to address the complex communication, behavioral, and learning needs of many clients, particularly those with autism spectrum disorder and other developmental disabilities.

For SLPs, this ethical mandate means more than simply being pleasant to colleagues from other disciplines. It requires actively seeking opportunities to share information, coordinate assessment and intervention approaches, and contribute your unique expertise to collaborative teams. When you encounter a student with significant behavioral challenges that impede communication therapy, the ethical response is not to work in isolation but to engage with the behavior analyst on the case.

Additionally, ASHA's code emphasizes the use of every resource, including referral and interprofessional collaboration, to ensure quality services are provided. Collaboration is not always easy, but it is what we are ethically called to do!

The BACB's ethical code includes several relevant standards for collaboration. Code 2.10 specifically addresses collaborating with colleagues, stating that behavior analysts collaborate with colleagues from their own and other professions in the best interest of clients.

They are expected to address conflicts by compromising when possible and always prioritizing the client's best interests.[2]

Code 3.06 discusses consulting with other providers, requiring behavior analysts to arrange for appropriate consultation with and referrals to other providers in the best interest of clients, with appropriate informed consent. This is particularly relevant when BCBAs work with students who have communication disorders or would benefit from augmentative and alternative communication (AAC) systems—areas where SLP expertise is essential.

Another critical ethical principle for behavior analysts is Code 2.08, which emphasizes using understandable language when communicating about services. This requirement helps address one of the most common barriers to effective collaboration: professional jargon. BCBAs are ethically obligated to communicate in ways that all team members, including parents and professionals from other disciplines, can understand.[3]

Understanding that both professions have explicit ethical obligations to collaborate provides a foundation for approaching interdisciplinary work not as an optional courtesy but as a professional responsibility. When challenges arise, you can return to these shared ethical principles as common ground.

One of the most significant barriers to effective collaboration is the lack of understanding about what training and education professionals from other disciplines receive. As an SLP, you bring extensive knowledge about speech and language development, articulation and phonology, swallowing and feeding, voice disorders, and many other areas. However, you may have limited insight into what BCBAs and RBTs learn during their certification processes. This knowledge gap can lead to misunderstandings, unrealistic expectations, or failure to leverage each professional's unique strengths.

WHAT EVERYONE BRINGS TO THE TABLE

SLP

Let's first establish what you, as an SLP, bring to the collaborative table. Your undergraduate coursework likely included foundational courses in communication disorders, anatomy and physiology of the speech and hearing mechanism, typical language development, and phonetics. Your graduate program then provided intensive training in areas such as articulation and phonological disorders, language disorders across the lifespan, motor speech disorders, swallowing and dysphagia, voice disorders, fluency disorders, and augmentative and alternative communication.

Most SLP graduate programs require approximately two years of full-time study, including extensive clinical practicum hours supervised by licensed clinicians. After graduation, you completed a Clinical Fellowship Year (CFY), a nine-month mentored professional experience where you worked under supervision while being paid as a professional. Only after successfully completing your CFY and passing a national examination did you receive your Certificate of Clinical Competence from ASHA.

Importantly, many SLP graduate programs do not require dedicated coursework in autism spectrum disorder or applied behavior analysis. Your knowledge in these areas may have developed primarily through clinical experience, continuing education, or self-directed learning rather than formal academic training. This is an important point when working with BCBAs, who may assume you have more background in behavioral principles than you received in your graduate program.

BCBA

BCBAs follow different educational pathways to certification, which can make understanding their background more complex. The BACB certification process has evolved significantly over time, so the training BCBAs received varies based on when they were certified.

Current requirements typically include a master's degree (though some hold doctoral degrees), completion of specific coursework in behavior analysis, and extensive supervised fieldwork hours. The required coursework covers ethics and professional conduct, concepts and principles of behavior analysis, measurement and data analysis, experimental design, fundamental elements of behavior change, behavior assessment, and specific behavior change procedures.

Notably, BCBAs receive intensive training in a three-semester-hour course dedicated entirely to ethics, far more extensive ethics education than most SLP programs provide. They also receive rigorous training in single-subject research methodology, data collection systems, and functional behavior assessment. Their supervised fieldwork hours focus on implementing behavior analytic interventions with fidelity.

The BACB certification began in the late 1990s, making it a relatively young profession compared to speech-language pathology. Currently, there are approximately 75,000 BCBAs certified. This rapid growth reflects the increasing demand for applied behavior analysis services, particularly for individuals with autism spectrum disorder.

Critically, BCBA coursework does not typically include dedicated instruction in speech and language development, phonetics, or communication disorders. While BCBAs learn about teaching communication skills using behavioral principles, they may not have the depth of knowledge about typical and atypical speech-language development that you possess. This is why your expertise is so valuable on interdisciplinary teams.

RBT

RBTs represent a paraprofessional certification in behavior analysis and are increasingly common on therapy teams. Understanding their training is important because you may work with RBTs more frequently than with BCBAs, particularly in ABA clinic settings or when students receive in-home ABA services.

Currently, to become an RBT, individuals must be at least 18 years old with a high school diploma, complete a 40-hour training program, pass a background check, and demonstrate competency through an assessment. The 40-hour training covers measurement, assessment, skill acquisition, behavior reduction, documentation and reporting, and professional conduct and scope of practice.

RBTs work under the direct supervision of a BCBA or BCaBA (Board Certified Assistant Behavior Analyst) who is responsible for their work. They implement behavior intervention plans and skill acquisition programs but do not design them independently. The RBT certification was established in 2014, and there are now over 206,000 certified RBTs, a remarkable growth that reflects the expansion of ABA services.

For SLPs, it's important to understand that RBTs, despite their valuable role in implementing interventions, have significantly less training than either BCBAs or SLPs. They should not be expected to make clinical decisions about communication interventions or modify programs independently. However, they can be excellent partners in generalizing the skills you target in therapy if given appropriate training and support.

BARRIERS TO COLLABORATION

Even with the best intentions and clear ethical mandates, several predictable barriers can impede collaboration between SLPs, BCBAs, and RBTs. Recognizing these obstacles is the first step toward addressing them proactively.

Language

Perhaps the most ubiquitous barrier is the use of profession-specific terminology. As an SLP, you may reference a student's mean length of utterance (MLU), phonological processes, or pragmatic language skills. When you use these terms with BCBAs or RBTs who haven't received training in communication disorders, they may not fully understand what you mean, even if they don't say so.

Similarly, BCBAs may discuss mands, tacts, echoics, antecedent interventions, or differential reinforcement procedures, terms from the behavioral lexicon that may be unfamiliar to you. An RBT might mention implementing a discrete trial training program or taking ABC data, using terminology you may not have encountered in your graduate training.

This jargon barrier creates several problems. First, it can make team members feel incompetent or defensive. When someone uses jargon in a meeting, you may feel embarrassed to ask for clarification, leading to nods of false understanding. Second, it wastes time and creates miscommunication. Team members may think they agree on a plan when they have different interpretations based on their understanding of the terminology. Finally, excessive jargon can make parents and other team members feel excluded from conversations about their own children.

Theory

SLPs and BCBAs may approach communication intervention from different theoretical frameworks, which can lead to philosophical disagreements about treatment approaches. For example, many SLPs embrace naturalistic, play-based intervention models that emphasize following the child's lead and embedding learning opportunities in meaningful activities. Meanwhile, some BCBAs may favor more structured, adult-directed teaching approaches with clearly defined trials and reinforcement contingencies.

Recent developments in the field have introduced additional complexity. The growing interest in gestalt language processing represents one area where SLPs and BCBAs may have divergent perspectives. Some SLPs are enthusiastically adopting gestalt language processing frameworks, while many BCBAs question the empirical foundation for this approach. These philosophical differences can create tension if not addressed thoughtfully.

Similarly, debates about augmentative and alternative communication can arise. Questions about when to introduce AAC, whether to continue working on verbal imitation, and how to balance core vocabulary versus fringe vocabulary can become contentious if team members approach these questions from rigid, opposing positions rather than collaborative problem-solving.

Scope

A critical distinction that often causes conflict is the difference between scope of practice and scope of competence. Your scope of practice as an SLP is defined by your license and encompasses the activities you are authorized to perform. However, your scope of competence refers to the activities within your scope of practice that you can perform competently based on your training and experience.

For example, dysphagia assessment and treatment may be within your scope of practice, but if you have never worked in medical settings or received specialized training in swallowing disorders, it may not be within your scope of competence. Conversely, a BCBA with extensive experience and training in AAC may have considerable competence in this area, even though it's more traditionally associated with SLP practice.

Conflicts often arise in overlapping areas where both professions may have expertise. Teaching verbal imitation skills, supporting communication development, and implementing AAC are all areas where SLPs and BCBAs may both work. Rather than viewing these overlaps as territorial disputes, successful teams recognize that each professional brings unique strengths to these shared domains and collaborate to leverage both perspectives.

PRACTICAL: TIME, STRUCTURE, ACCESS

Beyond philosophical differences, practical barriers can impede collaboration. In many settings, particularly schools, professionals have limited time built into their schedules for collaborative meetings. You may see students for 30-minute sessions throughout the day with no breaks between clients, making it nearly impossible to connect with the BCBA or RBT working with the same student.

Employment structures can also create barriers. You might be a direct employee of a school district while the BCBA is an outside consultant who visits periodically. Or you may work in a clinic where speech therapy is a billable service, but collaborative meetings are not, creating financial disincentives for collaboration.

Additionally, some therapy settings, particularly ABA clinics, may not have SLPs on staff or may only contract with SLPs on a limited basis. When BCBAs want to collaborate but don't have regular access to SLP expertise, they may make decisions about communication goals that would benefit from SLP input. Similarly, school-based SLPs may want to collaborate with outside ABA providers but have no clear mechanism for doing so.

Strategies

While barriers to collaboration are real, research and clinical experience have identified concrete strategies that significantly improve interdisciplinary teamwork. The following approaches, drawn from both professional literature and successful collaborative practices, can help you build more effective partnerships with BCBAs and RBTs.

Reach Out

Successful collaboration begins with basic relationship building. If a student on your caseload also receives ABA services, take the initiative to introduce yourself to the BCBA and any RBTs working with that student. This doesn't need to be elaborate—a brief email or a quick conversation when you see them in the school can establish the foundation for future collaboration. I know that it can seem difficult or overwhelming to do but this sets a good foundation for future collaboration. Or on the other hand if they reach out to you first, replying sets the stage for open and active correspondence.

Communication expectations early. Let the BCBA know you would appreciate being included in relevant meetings and that you're open to questions about communication goals. Offer to share your evaluation results and progress notes if requested to do so. If you work in a setting where direct communication is possible, suggest a regular check-in time, even if it's just 15 minutes monthly. Another great way to correspond is asynchronously. I have done this with shared Google Drive docs that allow for ongoing communication about client progress, and specific targets, for example.

Remember that ongoing communication is especially critical during times of difficulty. When a student isn't making progress or when you disagree about an intervention approach, resist the temptation to vent to colleagues and avoid addressing the issue directly. Instead, request a meeting, express your concerns professionally, and work toward a collaborative solution. These challenging conversations, while uncomfortable, are essential for professional growth and better serve your clients. Requesting a meeting will also depend on the work relationship of the BCBA, this request will vary depending on if they are an employee at the same school or clinic versus if they are a contractor. I also like to loop in my admin or special education director so that they know about any potential conflicts before they get bigger.

Use Plain Language

Commit to minimizing jargon in interdisciplinary settings. When you're in a meeting with BCBAs, RBTs, parents, and other professionals, assume that not everyone has the same background knowledge you do. Instead of saying a student has a phonological disorder characterized by cluster reduction and final consonant deletion, you might explain that the student has difficulty producing certain speech sounds and leaves off sounds at the ends of words.

When someone else uses unfamiliar terminology, ask for clarification. You might say, "I want to make sure I understand exactly what you mean by that. Could you explain it in different terms?" This models appropriate communication behavior and signals to others that it's safe to ask questions.

Similarly, when BCBAs use behavioral terminology, gently redirect them to more accessible language. If a BCBA says they're working on mands, you might respond, "So you're teaching requesting skills; that connects well with the functional communication goals I'm addressing in speech therapy." This demonstrates understanding while also translating for anyone who might not be familiar with the term *mand*. At times professionals may use this jargon without even realizing it!

Coordinate Assessments

Whenever possible, coordinate assessment activities with BCBAs working with your clients. If you're conducting a speech-language evaluation, share your results with the BCBA and ask about their assessment findings. You might discover that the BCBA administered an echoic assessment (verbal imitation test) as part of a VB-MAPP or ABLLS-R, which can provide valuable information about the student's ability to imitate speech sounds and words.

Conversely, share your standardized test results and clinical observations with the behavior analyst. If you've completed an articulation test, explain what the results mean for functional communication and how they might inform behavior programs. If you've assessed receptive language skills, discuss how these impact the student's ability to follow directions in ABA therapy sessions.

This collaborative assessment approach prevents duplication of effort, provides a more comprehensive picture of the student's abilities, and establishes a foundation for coordinated intervention planning. It also demonstrates mutual respect for each professional's expertise.

Create Shared Documentation Systems

One highly effective strategy is developing shared data collection or documentation systems. In school settings, this might mean creating a single data binder where all professionals working with a student can record progress on various goals. In clinic settings, it might involve shared digital platforms where everyone can access session notes and data.

For example, if you're working on speech sound production goals and the student receives ABA services during the week, you might create a simple data sheet that RBTs can use to practice targeted words during maintenance activities. This allows the student more opportunities to practice between speech sessions and helps generalize skills across settings and people.

Shared documentation also promotes transparency and accountability. When everyone can see what others are working on, it's easier to identify overlaps, gaps, or opportunities for integration. It also provides clear evidence of collaborative practice, which may be important for insurance documentation, Individual Education Plan (IEP) compliance, or quality improvement initiatives.

Distinguish and Respect Professional Roles

Take time early in your collaborative relationships to clarify each team member's competencies and areas of expertise. You might say something like, "I have extensive experience with AAC and would be happy to lead device programming and family training in that area." Or, "I don't have much experience with students who engage in self-injurious behavior, so I would really value your guidance on safety protocols and behavioral strategies."

This clarity helps prevent assumptions and misunderstandings. It also opens the door for role expansion and role release, concepts from interprofessional collaboration research. Role expansion occurs when a professional learns to perform tasks typically associated with another discipline under appropriate supervision. Role release involves strategically allowing another professional to take the lead in an area where they have expertise.

For example, you might teach an experienced RBT to implement specific articulation practice activities you've designed, expanding their role while maintaining your oversight. Conversely, you might release some behavioral management strategies to the BCBA's expertise, trusting their recommendations even when they differ from your initial approach.

Develop Shared Problem-solving Protocols

When conflicts or disagreements arise, and they inevitably will, having a shared framework for resolution is invaluable. Dr. Matthew Broadhead's decision-making model for addressing disagreements about interventions provides an excellent template.[4] The framework asks several key questions:

- Is client safety at risk?
- Are you familiar with the proposed treatment?
- Can the treatment be translated into your professional framework?
- Will it negatively interfere with the client's goals?
- Are the potential impacts sufficient to justify compromising the professional relationship?

This structured approach prevents emotional reactions and helps teams focus on the most important consideration: the client's best interest. For example, if a BCBA proposes an intervention approach you're unfamiliar with, the first step is to learn more about it rather than reflexively objecting. If after learning about it you still have concerns, articulate them specifically in relation to client safety and goal achievement rather than simply stating it conflicts with your preferred approach.

Agree as a team that when disagreements occur, you'll address them directly through scheduled meetings rather than through email exchanges, which can easily escalate tensions. Commit to assuming positive intent, recognizing that your colleagues genuinely want what's best for students, even when you disagree about methods.

CLINICAL AREAS OF OVERLAP

Certain clinical areas frequently become points of contention between SLPs and BCBAs because they fall within the overlapping scopes of both professions. Understanding how to approach these areas collaboratively is essential for effective teamwork.

Augmentative and Alternative Communication (AAC)

AAC is perhaps the area where SLPs and BCBAs struggle to collaborate. SLPs typically have more extensive training in AAC systems, device features, and language representation methods. However, BCBAs bring valuable expertise in teaching communication skills systematically, generalizing skills across settings, and integrating AAC into behavioral programming.

A collaborative approach recognizes that the AAC device belongs to the client, not to any one professional. As one dually certified SLP/BCBA aptly stated, "This isn't the BCBA's device. This isn't the speech therapist's device. This device belongs to the client." This perspective shift is crucial.

Best practice involves having the SLP lead the AAC assessment, device selection, and initial programming decisions, given their specialized training. However, this leadership should involve consultation with the BCBA about the student's behavioral needs, learning style, and reinforcement preferences. Once a device is selected, both professionals should collaborate on vocabulary selection, teaching strategies, and generalization planning.

Training RBTs and other team members to support AAC use is essential but should not involve creating folder systems or separate materials that bypass the actual device. Such practices, unfortunately common in some settings, undermine the purpose of AAC and contribute to device abandonment. Instead, focus on training team members to model device use, honor communication attempts, and integrate the device throughout the student's day.

Teaching Verbal Imitation

Teaching verbal imitation represents another area of frequent overlap. BCBAs often work on echoic skills (behavioral term for verbal imitation) as part of language acquisition programs. However, SLPs bring critical expertise about speech sound development, articulation, and the motor planning required for speech production.

A collaborative approach might work as follows: The BCBA administers an echoic assessment to determine which sounds, syllables, and words the student can imitate. The SLP administers a standardized articulation test to identify specific speech sound errors and patterns. Together, you analyze both sets of results to create a comprehensive picture of the student's verbal imitation abilities and speech production skills.

From there, the SLP takes the lead on teaching new speech sounds or correcting error patterns in therapy sessions, working on targets until the student achieves criterion. Once sounds or words are mastered in speech therapy, they are placed in maintenance, with RBTs or BCBAs incorporating them into ongoing activities and programs. This division of labor leverages each professional's strengths while providing the student with maximal practice opportunities.

The key is recognizing that working on verbal imitation doesn't preclude also using AAC. A total communication approach that includes verbal speech, sign language, and aided AAC provides the most robust support for communication development. Neither professional should insist that a student must master verbal skills before introducing AAC or that introducing AAC means abandoning work on speech production.

Gestalt language processing has emerged as an area of significant interest and, sometimes, controversy. This framework proposes that some individuals learn language by first acquiring and using multi-word chunks (gestalts) before gradually breaking them down into smaller units and eventually generating novel utterances.

Many SLPs have embraced this framework and attend training on supporting gestalt language processors. However, many SLPs and BCBAs often express concern about the limited empirical research base for gestalt language processing interventions. A recent systematic review found an apparent lack of treatment studies examining or supporting this approach, leading to questions about its evidence base.

When navigating this area collaboratively, first seek to understand each other's perspectives. If you're implementing a gestalt language processing approach, explain the framework to your colleagues, share the clinical reasoning behind your approach, and discuss how you're measuring progress. Be transparent about the current state of research while also noting that many effective clinical practices began with observation and clinical experience before controlled studies established their efficacy.

Conversely, if a BCBA questions your use of a gestalt approach, consider their concerns seriously rather than dismissing them as ignorance of current SLP practice. Many therapeutic principles associated with gestalt language processing, building on the student's current language system, honoring communication attempts, following the child's interests, are consistent with best practices regardless of theoretical framework. You may find common ground by focusing on these shared principles rather than debating the gestalt model itself.

Most importantly, always prioritize client safety and functional outcomes over adherence to any model. If a student needs to learn personal safety information like their name, address, or how to ask for help, these goals should be addressed even if they don't align perfectly with stage-based gestalt language processing recommendations. The student's needs are what should be our main focus.

SALAD, STEW, OR CAKE?

Research on interprofessional collaboration describes a continuum from multidisciplinary to interdisciplinary to transdisciplinary practice. A memorable way to think about this continuum uses food metaphors: Are you a salad, a stew, or a cake?

Multidisciplinary practice (salad) involves professionals working in parallel with minimal communication, each focusing on discipline-specific tasks. You provide speech therapy, the BCBA provides ABA services, but you rarely interact. Like salad ingredients, each component is identifiable and separate.

Interdisciplinary practice (stew) includes coordinated tasks with frequent communication, shared goals and responsibilities, though discipline roles are maintained. You meet regularly, share information, and coordinate your approaches while each maintaining your professional identity. Like stew ingredients, elements blend but remain somewhat distinct.

Transdisciplinary practice (cake) involves role release, role expansion, integrated expertise, shared problem-solving, and unified treatment plans. Team members cross traditional professional boundaries when appropriate, teach each other specialized skills, and create truly integrated interventions. Like a cake, individual ingredients combine to create something that transcends its component parts.

Most teams realistically operate somewhere between stew and cake, with the specific level of integration depending on the client's needs, the team's history of working together, and organizational supports for collaboration. The goal is not necessarily to always achieve cake-level integration but to intentionally move beyond salad-level isolation toward more coordinated and integrated practice.

Effective collaboration between speech-language pathologists, board certified behavior analysts, and registered behavior technicians is not merely a pleasant professional courtesy; rather, it is an ethical imperative grounded in both professions' codes of conduct. When we collaborate successfully, we leverage the unique strengths of each discipline to provide more comprehensive, effective services than any single professional could offer alone.

This chapter has explored the ethical foundations for collaboration, examined the different educational backgrounds that shape each profession's perspective, identified common barriers to effective teamwork, and provided concrete strategies for building strong interdisciplinary partnerships. You now have both the conceptual understanding and practical tools to enhance your collaborative relationships.

The reality is that collaboration is often challenging. It requires time, effort, flexibility, and a willingness to have difficult conversations. You will encounter BCBAs whose approaches differ markedly from yours. You will experience frustration when organizational structures don't support the collaboration you know would benefit your students. You will face situations where compromise feels uncomfortable.

However, the alternative of working in isolation serves no one well, least of all the children and families who depend on our expertise. When speech-language pathologists and behavior analysts work together effectively, students with autism and other developmental disabilities achieve outcomes neither profession could produce alone. Communication skills generalize more successfully. Behavioral challenges decrease more rapidly. Families feel more supported and less overwhelmed by conflicting professional advice.

As you return to your clinical practice, commit to taking at least one concrete action to enhance collaboration. Perhaps you'll reach out to a BCBA you've never met who works with one of your students. Maybe you'll develop a shared data collection system or propose a monthly collaborative meeting time. You might commit to asking for clarification when you hear unfamiliar jargon rather than nodding in false understanding. Or you could volunteer to lead a lunch-and-learn session for RBTs about speech and language development.

Whatever action you choose, remember that building strong collaborative relationships is a process, not an event. You won't transform your workplace culture overnight, but consistent, incremental efforts accumulate over time. Each small act of reaching out, clarifying, coordinating, and problem solving together moves your team along the continuum from salad toward cake.

The students we serve deserve nothing less than our best collaborative efforts. They need SLPs who understand behavior, BCBAs who value communication, and teams that work together seamlessly to support both domains. By committing to ethical, informed, and skilled collaboration, you honor your professional responsibilities and, more importantly, provide the comprehensive, coordinated services that can truly change lives.

The journey from practicing in isolation to collaborative practice begins with a single step. What will yours be? Reach out and let me know! Message me on Instagram @abaspeechbyrose or at my site www.abaspeech.org, I read each and every message!

NOTES

1. American Speech-Language-Hearing Association. (2023). Code of Ethics [Ethics]. Available from www.asha.org/policy/.
2. Behavior Analyst Certification Board. (2020). Ethics code for behavior analysts. https://bacb.com/wp-content/ethics-code-for-behavior-analysts/.
3. Bowman, K. S., Suarez, V. D., & Weiss, M. J. (2021). Standards for interprofessional collaboration in the treatment of individuals with autism. *Behavior Analysis in Practice*, *14*(4), 1191–1208. https://doi.org/10.1007/s40617-021-00560-0.
4. Brodhead M. T. (2015). Maintaining professional relationships in an interdisciplinary setting: strategies for navigating nonbehavioral treatment recommendations for individuals with autism. *Behavior Analysis in Practice*, *8*(1), 70–78. https://doi.org/10.1007/s40617-015-0042-7.

Appendix A: Receptive ID Activities

Receptive ID Items—Preschool Special Education

Category	Examples
Common Animals	Dog, Cat, Cow, Duck, Pig
Body Parts	Nose, Hands, Feet, Eyes, Ears
Clothing Items	Shoes, Hat, Coat, Shirt, Pants
Toys	Ball, Car, Doll, Blocks, Puzzle
Food Items	Apple, Cookie, Banana, Cracker, Juice
Colors	Red, Blue, Yellow, Green, Purple
Shapes	Circle, Square, Triangle, Star, Heart
Furniture/Classroom	Chair, Table, Book, Crayon, Backpack
People	Teacher, Mom, Dad, Friend, Baby
Vehicles	Car, Bus, Airplane, Train, Truck

1. **Receptive Identification of an Action (in an array of three cards)**
   - Show me jumping.
   - Show me sleeping.
   - Show me eating.
   - Show me running.
   - Show me hugging.
   - Show me brushing teeth.
   - Show me dancing.
   - Show me waving.
   - Show me crying.
   - Show me playing.

2. **Receptive Identification Based on Function**
   - Which one do you eat with? (spoon)
   - Which one do you wear on your feet? (shoes)
   - Which one do you drink from? (cup)
   - What do you write? (crayon)
   - Which one do you sleep on? (bed)
   - What do you talk on? (phone)
   - Which one do you cut with? (scissors)
   - What do you open a door with? (key)
   - Which one keeps you dry in the rain? (umbrella)
   - Which one do you play? (piano)

3. **Receptive Identification Based on Features**
   - Which one is round? (ball)
   - Which one is red? (apple)
   - Which one is soft? (pillow)
   - Which one is big? (elephant)
   - Which one is small? (mouse)
   - Which one has wheels? (car)
   - Which one is cold? (ice)
   - Which one is loud? (drum)
   - Which one has a beak? (bird)
   - Which one is hot? (sun)

4. **Filling in the Blank for Common Phrases**
   - Ready, set ... **go!**
   - Twinkle, twinkle little ... **star**
   - Row, row, row your ... **boat**
   - A, B, C ... **D**
   - The wheels on the ... **bus**
   - Old MacDonald had a ... **farm**
   - Up above the world so ... **high**
   - Brush your ... **teeth**

- 1, 2, 3 ... **4**
- A cat says ... **meow**

---

5. **Answering Personal Safety Questions**
   - What's your name?
   - What is your address?
   - What's your mom's name?
   - What's your dad's name?
   - What's your phone number?

---

6. **Answering "WH" Questions Within a Book (with visual)**
   - Who is riding the bike?
   - What is the bear eating?
   - Where is the girl going?
   - When does the story happen? (day/night)
   - Why is the boy sad?
   - What is the character holding?
   - Who is in the tree?
   - What color is the dog?
   - Where is the ball?
   - Why did the girl cry?

---

7. **Answering Social Language Questions (with visual)**
   - What breakfast food do you like?
   - What sport do you like to play?
   - What instrument do you like to play?
   - What is your favorite color?
   - What dessert do you like to eat?
   - What holiday do you like?
   - What animal do you like to see at the zoo?
   - Where would you want to go on vacation?
   - What do you like to do for fun?
   - What is your favorite season?

Appendix B: Key Questions for Parents of Nonspeaking Autistic Children

Communication Attempts and Methods

1. How does your child currently let you know what they want or need?
2. What types of sounds, gestures, or behaviors does your child use to communicate with you?
3. Does your child use any consistent gestures, signs, pictures, or other methods to communicate?
4. In what situations is your child most likely to try to communicate with you or others?

Communication Understanding

5. How do you know when your child understands what you're saying?
6. What types of directions or requests does your child seem to understand consistently?
7. How does your child respond when you call their name?
8. Does your child seem to understand more than they can express? If so, how can you tell?

Social Communication

9. Does your child try to get your attention to show you things they find interesting? If so, how?
10. How does your child respond when you're trying to engage them in play or conversation?
11. Does your child engage in any back-and-forth interactions, such as games like peek-a-boo or taking turns?
12. Who does your child seem most comfortable communicating with and why do you think that is?

Communication History and Development

13. Has your child ever used words or word approximations? If so, which ones and in what contexts?

14. Have you noticed any regression or loss of communication skills your child previously had?

15. What has been most effective in helping your child communicate so far?

Motivations and Preferences

16. What activities, toys, or topics seem to interest or motivate your child the most?

17. Are there specific situations where your child seems more likely to attempt communication?

Family Context and Goals

18. What are your biggest concerns about your child's communication right now?

19. What are your hopes or goals for your child's communication development in the next 6–12 months?

20. What communication strategies have you tried at home, and what has been most successful?

Appendix C: Group Data Sheet

Activities: _______________________________

Date: ___________________________________

Student	Skill	Data	Skill	Data
		+ –		+ –
		+ –		+ –
		+ –		+ –
		+ –		+ –
		+ –		+ –

Appendix D: ABC Data Sheet

Date____ / ____ / ____

Date	Time	Antecedent	Behavior	Consequence	Staff Member

Appendix E: Informal Assessments

COMMUNICATION SCREENER
PRE-SCHOOL

General Information

Child Name

Child Birthday

Screener Date

Person Completing

General Communication

How is your child currently communicating?

☐ Talking   ☐ Pointing and Gestures   ☐ Bringing you to the item(s) they want?

Social Engagement:

Will your child sit by you when you read a book?	Yes	No
Will your child sit by you to play with toys?	Yes	No
Will your child help you with routines around the house?	Yes	No

Requesting:

How does your child let you know they want something or that they want to do something?

Matching:

Is your child able to do simple puzzles?	Yes	No
Is your child able to match the same items or pictures?	Yes	No

Play:

Does your child enjoy playing with toys?	Yes	No
Does your child enjoy playing with a variety of toys?	Yes	No
Will your child explore new toys?	Yes	No
Does your child enjoy play activities?	Yes	No

COMMUNICATION SCREENER

General Communication

Play Continued:

What toys does your child currently enjoy playing with?
What play activities does your child currently enjoy?

Following One Step Directions:

Is your child able to follow simple one step directions?   Yes   No
(i.e. get your shoes, give that to mommy, get your blanket)

Labeling:

Is your child able to label items?   Yes   No

Is your child able to label actions?   Yes   No

Filling In The Blanks:

Is your child able to fill in the blank for familiar phrases?   Yes   No
(i.e. Ready, Set, _______ or A, B, C, _____)

Imitation:

Is your child able to imitate actions?   Yes   No

Is your child able to imitate actions with objects?   Yes   No

Is your child able to imitate sounds or words?   Yes   No

Spontaneous Communication

If your child is spontaneously communicating - note specific examples below.

Other Notes:

COMMUNICATION SCREENER
SCHOOL AGE

General Information

Child Name

Child Birthday

Screener Date

Person Completing

General Communication

How is your child currently communicating?

☐ Talking   ☐ Pointing and Gestures   ☐ Bringing you to the item(s) they want?

Social Engagement:

Will your child sit by you when you read a book?	Yes	No
Will your child sit by you to play with toys?	Yes	No
Will your child help you with routines around the house?	Yes	No

Requesting:

How does your child let you know they want something or that they want to do something?

Matching:

Is your child able to do simple puzzles?	Yes	No
Is your child able to match the same items or pictures?	Yes	No

Play:

Does your child enjoy playing with toys?	Yes	No
Does your child enjoy playing with a variety of toys?	Yes	No
Will your child explore new toys?	Yes	No
Does your child enjoy play activities?	Yes	No

COMMUNICATION SCREENER

General Communication

Play Continued:

What toys does your child currently enjoy playing with?
What play activities does your child currently enjoy?

Following One Step Directions:

Is your child able to follow simple one step directions?   Yes   No
(i.e. get your shoes, give that to mommy, get your blanket)

Labeling:

Is your child able to label items?   Yes   No

Is your child able to label actions?   Yes   No

Filling In The Blanks:

Is your child able to fill in the blank for familiar phrases?   Yes   No
(i.e. Ready, Set, _______ or A, B, C, _____)

Imitation:

Is your child able to imitate actions?   Yes   No

Is your child able to imitate actions with objects?   Yes   No

Is your child able to imitate sounds or words?   Yes   No

Spontaneous Communication

If your child is spontaneously communicating - note specific examples below.

Other Notes:

COMMUNICATION SCREENER
ADVANCED LANGUAGE LEARNER

General Information

Child Name

Child Birthday

Screener Date

Person Completing

General Communication

How is your student currently communicating?

Expressive Language:

Can the student label a variety of nouns?   Yes   No

Can the student label a variety of actions?   Yes   No

Grammatical Markers:

What grammatical markers does the student use in structured and spontaneous communication activities?

Vocabulary:

Is the student able to list 3 critical features of functional terms?   Yes   No

Is the student able to list 3 critical features of curricular terms?   Yes   No

Comprehension:

Does the student answer functional who questions?   Yes   No

Does the student answer functional what questions?   Yes   No

Does the student answer functional where questions?   Yes   No

Does the student answer personal safety questions?   Yes   No

After reading a level appropriate passage can the student answer a variety   Yes   No
of "WH" questions?

COMMUNICATION SCREENER

General Communication

Following Directions:

Is your student able to follow one-step directions in the larger school environment?	Yes	No
Is your student able to follow two-step directions in the larger school environment?	Yes	No
Is your student able to follow one-step directions with a paper/pencil task?	Yes	No
Is your student able to follow two-step directions with a paper/pencil task?	Yes	No

Social Language:

Is your student able to engage in parallel play?	Yes	No
Is your student able to initiate play when they want to play with another peer?	Yes	No
Is your student able to engage in a group activity for 15 minutes?	Yes	No
Is your student able to engage in a group activity for 30 minutes?	Yes	No
Is your student able to participate 5 times in a group activity?	Yes	No

Speech Clarity:

What speech sounds does your student have difficulty producing?

Other Notes:

COMMUNICATION SCREENER

Observation At Lunch & Recess

Observation In An Academic Class Small Group

Observation In An Academic Class Large Group

Observation In A Specials Class

Appendix F: Autism IEP Goal Bank

AUTISM GOALS ACROSS THE LIFESPAN FROM ABA SPEECH

AUTISM GOAL BANK

Early Learner Skills

- Student will engage in a shared literacy-based activity for a duration of 3 minutes, without prompts, over 2 consecutive sessions.
- Student will engage in a shared movement-based activity for a duration of 3 minutes, without prompts, over 2 consecutive sessions.
- Student will engage in a shared play-based activity for a duration of 3 minutes, without prompts, over 2 consecutive sessions.
- Student will engage in a shared music -based activity for a duration of 3 minutes, without prompts, over 2 consecutive sessions.

Receptive Language Skills

- Student will follow functional one-step directions with 90% accuracy, over 2 consecutive sessions.
- Student will point to or touch pictures of preferred items, people and places, when presented in an array of 3 with 90% accuracy, over 2 consecutive sessions.
- Student will match identical items, without prompts, over 2 consecutive sessions.
- Student will match identical pictures, without prompts, over 2 consecutive sessions.

Play Skills

- The student will engage in independent play with a preferred toy for a duration of 3 minutes, without prompts, over 2 consecutive sessions.
- The student will engage in independent play with a less familiar toy for a duration of 3 minutes, without prompts, over 2 consecutive sessions.
- The student will engage in movement-based play for a duration of 3 minutes, without prompts, over 2 consecutive sessions.
- The student will engage in parallel play near other children, for a duration of 3 minutes, without prompts, over 2 consecutive sessions.

AUTISM GOALS ACROSS THE LIFESPAN FROM ABA SPEECH

AUTISM GOAL BANK CONT.

Imitation

- The student will imitate gross motor movements, when shown a movement by the instructor, without prompts, over 2 consecutive sessions.
- The student will imitate actions taking place during a play-based activity when shown an action by the instructor, without prompts, over 2 consecutive sessions.
- Given a therapist model, the student will imitate functional one-syllable words, with 90% accuracy, over 2 consecutive sessions.
- Given a therapist model, the student will imitate functional two-syllable words, with 90% accuracy, over 2 consecutive sessions.

Expressive Language Skills

- Student will request specific items or actions without prompts, over 2 consecutive sessions.
- Student will label preferred items when shown a picture with 90% accuracy, over 2 consecutive sessions.
- Student will label functional Items when shown a picture, with 90% accuracy, over 2 consecutive sessions.
- Student will label actions when shown a picture or the actual action, with 90% accuracy, over 2 consecutive sessions.

AUTISM GOALS ACROSS THE LIFESPAN FROM ABA SPEECH

ADVANCED LANGUAGE LEARNER GOAL BANK

Receptive Language

- The student will increase their overall receptive language skills by identifying items by their feature without prompts, over 2 consecutive sessions.
- The student will increase their overall receptive language skills by identifying items by their function without prompts, over 2 consecutive sessions.
- The student will increase their overall receptive language skills by identifying items by their class without prompts, over 2 consecutive sessions.
- The student will increase their overall receptive language skills by identifying items by adjectives, adverbs and associations with 90% accuracy, over 2 consecutive sessions.
- When presented with a field of 3 pictures and given a picture and the direction "Match (targeted item), the student will match to the correct category without prompts, over 2 consecutive sessions.
- The student will increase their overall receptive language skills by selecting the correct item from a book when given a "wh question" without prompts, over 2 consecutive sessions.

Following Directions

- The student will increase their overall receptive language skills by following one-step directions that include prepositions without prompts, over 2 consecutive sessions.
- The student will increase their overall receptive language skills by following one-step directions during a paper/pencil task without prompts, over 2 consecutive sessions.
- The student will increase their overall receptive language skills by following one-step directions in the larger school environment without prompts, over 3 consecutive sessions.
- The student will increase their overall receptive language skills by following two-step directions in the larger school environment without prompts, over 3 consecutive sessions.

Page 3 of 18

AUTISM GOALS ACROSS THE LIFESPAN FROM ABA SPEECH

ADVANCED LANGUAGE LEARNER GOAL BANK CONT.

Comprehension

- The student will answer functional who questions with 90% accuracy, over 3 consecutive sessions.
- The student will answer functional what questions with 90% accuracy, over 3 consecutive sessions.
- The student will answer functional where questions with 90% accuracy, over 3 consecutive sessions.
- The student will answer functional when questions with 90% accuracy, over 3 consecutive sessions.
- The student will answer personal safety questions without prompts, over 2 consecutive sessions.
- After reading a level-appropriate reading passage, the student will answer 5 questions with 90% accuracy, over 2 consecutive sessions.

Speech Clarity

- The student will imitate 2 syllable functional words after a clinician's model, without prompts, over 3 consecutive sessions.
- The student will imitate 3 syllable functional words after a clinician's model, without prompts, over 3 consecutive sessions.
- The student will imitate 2-word combinations after a clinician's model, without prompts, over 3 consecutive sessions.
- The student will produce the (targeted speech sound) in the initial, medial and final positions of words with 90% accuracy over 3 consecutive sessions.
- The student will produce the (targeted speech sound) in the initial, medial and final positions of words in sentences with 90% accuracy, over 3 consecutive sessions.
- The student will produce the (targeted speech sound) in spontaneous communication with 90% accuracy, across 2 consecutive sessions.

AUTISM GOALS ACROSS THE LIFESPAN FROM ABA SPEECH

ADVANCED LANGUAGE LEARNER GOAL BANK CONT.

Expressive Language

- The student will increase his overall expressive language skills by using two word requests (a total of 20 in a 60-minute observation) independently, over 3 consecutive sessions.
- The student will imitate 3 syllable functional words after a clinician's model, without prompts, over 3 consecutive sessions.
- When presented with a picture of an action taking place, the student will create a two-word phrase to describe the picture with 90% accuracy, over 3 consecutive sessions.
- When presented with a picture of an action taking place, the student will create a grammatically correct sentence to describe the picture with 90% accuracy, over 3 consecutive sessions.
- The student will increase his overall expressive language skills by using grammatical markers within a structured activity with 90% accuracy, over 3 consecutive sessions.
- The student will increase his overall expressive language skills by using the correct irregular past tense verb form with 90% accuracy, over 3 consecutive sessions.
- The student will increase her overall expressive language skills by labeling 4 prepositions correctly without prompts, over 2 consecutive sessions.
- The student will increase her overall expressive language skills by labeling functional curricular terms correctly with 90% accuracy, over 2 consecutive sessions.
- The student will increase her overall expressive language skills by listing three critical elements of a presented word without prompts, over 3 consecutive sessions. correctly without prompts, over 2 consecutive sessions.

Self Monitoring

- The student will independently describe the targeted skill that they are working on in therapy, over 2 consecutive sessions.
- The student will take data on the use of a targeted skill without prompts, over 3 consecutive sessions.

Page 5 of 18

AUTISM GOALS ACROSS THE LIFESPAN FROM ABA SPEECH

ADVANCED LANGUAGE LEARNER GOAL BANK CONT.

Social Language

- The student will engage in parallel play near other children for a duration of 5 minutes, without prompts, over 2 consecutive sessions.
- The student will initiate a play activity with another child two times during a 30 minute observation without prompting, over 2 consecutive sessions.
- The student will engage in play activities with another peer or peers for a duration of 5 minutes without prompting, over 2 consecutive sessions.
- The student will engage in a cooperative play activity with another child for a duration of 5 minutes, without prompts, over 2 consecutive sessions.
- The student will participate in a small group activity for 5 minutes and attend to the teacher, without prompts, over 2 consecutive sessions.
- The student will respond to 4 different group instructions without prompts, over 2 consecutive sessions.
- The student will answer a social question when asked by a peer without prompts (a total of 4 questions) over 2 consecutive sessions.
- The student will initiate conversation on a topic of their choice (a total of 5) without prompts, over 2 consecutive sessions.
- The student will participate expressively 10 times during a 25 minute group, without prompts, over 2 consecutive sessions.
- The student will participate 5 times during a small group activity 25 minutes in duration, without prompts, over 2 consecutive sessions.
- The student will participate 10 times during a small group activity 25 minutes in duration, without prompts, over 2 consecutive sessions.

Self Advocacy

- The student will request clarification as needed across the day with no more than 1 prompt, over 4 consecutive days.
- The student will learn 2 strategies for self-advocacy that can be used across their day by the end of the first quarter, without prompts.

Page 6 of 18

AUTISM GOALS ACROSS THE LIFESPAN FROM ABA SPEECH

SOCIAL SKILLS GOAL BANK

Social and Group Skills

- The student will engage in parallel play near other children for a duration of 5 minutes, without prompts, over 2 consecutive sessions.
- The student will initiate a play activity with another child two times during a 30 minute observation without prompting, over 2 consecutive sessions.
- The student will engage in play activities with another peer or peers for a duration of 5 minutes without prompting, over 2 consecutive sessions.
- The student will engage in a cooperative play activity with another child for a duration of 5 minutes, without prompts, over 2 consecutive sessions.
- The student will participate in a small group activity for 5 minutes and attend to the teacher, without prompts, over 2 consecutive sessions.
- The student will respond to 4 different group instructions without prompts, over 2 consecutive sessions.
- The student will answer a social question when asked by a peer without prompts (a total of 4 questions) over 2 consecutive sessions.
- The student will initiate conversation on a topic of their choice (a total of 5) without prompts, over 2 consecutive sessions.
- The student will participate expressively 10 times during a 25 minute group, without prompts, over 2 consecutive sessions.

AUTISM GOALS ACROSS THE LIFESPAN FROM ABA SPEECH

LIFE SKILLS GOAL BANK

Social Language Skills

- The student will engage in a cooperative leisure activity with another student for a duration of 5 minutes, without prompts, over 2 consecutive sessions.
- The student will participate in a small group activity for 15 minutes and attend to the teacher, without prompts, over 2 consecutive sessions.
- The student will respond to 4 different group instructions without prompts, over 2 consecutive sessions.
- The student will answer a social question when asked by a peer without prompts (a total of 4 questions) over 2 consecutive sessions.
- The student will initiate conversation on a topic of their choice (a total of 5) without prompts, over 2 consecutive sessions.
- The student will participate expressively 10 times during a 25 minute group, without prompts, over 2 consecutive sessions.

Expressive Language Skills

- The student will label vocational items without prompts, over 2 consecutive sessions without prompts.
- The student will label vocational actions without prompts, over 2 consecutive sessions without prompts.
- When presented with a functional vocabulary term, the student will label the item, describe the function and provide 2 other details about the item, without prompts, over 2 consecutive sessions.
- When presented with a 4 part story, the student will use a grammatically correct sentence about each picture depicted in the story, without prompts, over 2 consecutive sessions.
- When presented with a category, the student will name 3 members that belong to that category, without prompts, over 2 consecutive

AUTISM GOALS ACROSS THE LIFESPAN FROM ABA SPEECH

LIFE SKILLS GOAL BANK CONT.

Receptive Language Skills

- The student will answer 5 functional "wh" questions while performing a vocational task without prompts, over 2 consecutive sessions.
- The student will follow all items on a task analysis of a vocational task (making copies, doing recycling, etc...) with no more than 1 prompt, over 2 consecutive sessions.
- The student will follow all items on a task analysis of a leisure skill (setting up and playing modified uno, etc..) with no more than 1 prompt, over 2 consecutive sessions.
- The student will follow functional one step directions in the larger school environment (i.e "Please take this to the office) without prompts, over 2 consecutive sessions.
- The student will follow functional two step directions in the larger school environment (i.e "Please take this to the office and shred these papers) without prompts, over 2 consecutive sessions.

AUTISM GOALS ACROSS THE LIFESPAN FROM ABA SPEECH

GENERAL ACADEMICS

Math - Number Sense

- Learner will rote count to 20/50/100, etc. with 90% accuracy, across 3 consecutive sessions.
- Learner will point to requested number up to 10/20/50/100, etc. from a field of 2-6 with 90% accuracy, across 3 consecutive sessions.
- Learner will match numeral to corresponding set of objects up to 10, from a field of 2-6, with 90% accuracy, across 3 consecutive sessions.
- Learner will count a set of objects up to 5/10/20, with 90% accuracy, across 3 consecutive sessions.
- Learner will count out and exchange a requested number of items up to 5/10/20, with 90% accuracy, across 3 consecutive sessions.
- Given two sets of objects, learner will point to the set that is "more" or "less" when asked, with 90% accuracy, across 3 consecutive sessions.
- Given two numerals, learner will point to the numeral that is "more" or "less" when asked, with 90% accuracy, across 3 consecutive sessions.
- Learner will use language such as "more," "less," and "equal" to describe numerals' relationship to one another, with 90% accuracy, across 3 consecutive sessions.
- Learner will use add sums up to 5/10/20 using manipulatives, with 90% accuracy, across 3 consecutive sessions.

Math - Time Concepts

- Learner will use language such as "before" and "after" to describe events' relationship to one another, with 90% accuracy, across 3 consecutive sessions.
- Learner will sequence events of a day, with 90% accuracy, across 3 consecutive sessions.
- Learner will independently set a variety of timers to a requested amount of time within one minute of being asked, in 4/5 requested opportunities.
- Learner will transition between activities when timer alerts, with or without prompts, in 90% of opportunities for 4/5 consecutive school days.

AUTISM GOALS ACROSS THE LIFESPAN FROM ABA SPEECH

GENERAL ACADEMICS CONT.

Math - Money Concepts

- Learner will match coin or bill to value, with 90% accuracy, across 3 consecutive sessions.
- Learner will name coin or bill value, with 90% accuracy, across 3 consecutive sessions.
- Learner will select coin or bill from written/spoken value, with 90% accuracy, across 3 consecutive sessions.
- Learner will count coin combinations up to a value of $2.00, with 90% accuracy, across 3 consecutive sessions.
- Learner will count bill combinations up to a value of $10/$20/$50, with 90% accuracy, across 3 consecutive sessions.
- Learner will count bill and coin combinations up to a value of $10/$20/$50, with 90% accuracy, across 3 consecutive sessions.
- Learner will identify whether a given amount of money is enough to purchase an item labeled with a price, with 90% accuracy, across 3 consecutive sessions.

Reading Comprehension

- Learner will follow a recipe/cooking instructions with 5-10 steps, with or without picture support, completing 80% of steps independently for 3 consecutive opportunities for (#) different recipes.
- Learner will follow written instructions with 5-10 steps, with or without picture support, completing 80% of steps independently for 3 consecutive opportunities for (#) different functional tasks.
- Learner will answer literal comprehension questions (who, what, where, when, how) about a text read to self or read aloud by staff with 90% accuracy for 3 consecutive opportunities.
- Learner will answer inferential comprehension questions (why, what next, etc.) about a text read to self or read aloud by staff with 90% accuracy for 3 consecutive opportunities.

AUTISM GOALS ACROSS THE LIFESPAN FROM ABA SPEECH

GENERAL ACADEMICS CONT.

Reading Leisure

- Learner will look at book or magazine for increasing durations above baseline independently in 4/5 consecutive opportunities.
- Learner will select book/magazine from library or other collection, return to seating area and initiate browsing, completing 90% of task-analysis steps independently, in 4/5 opportunities.
- Learner will follow steps on visual checklist to access recorded book on youtube/CD recording/other audio modality, completing 90% of task-analysis steps independently, for 3 consecutive sessions.

Writing

- Learner will write 26/26 letters of the alphabet with 100% accuracy for 4 consecutive school days.
- Learner will independently write name with 100% accuracy in 4/5 opportunities for 4 consecutive school days.
- Learner will independently write name on work with 100% accuracy in 4/5 opportunities for 4 consecutive school days.
- Learner will use name stamp to label work with 100% accuracy in 4/5 opportunities for 4 consecutive school days.

AUTISM GOALS ACROSS THE LIFESPAN FROM ABA SPEECH

GENERAL ADLS

Classroom ADLs

- Upon arrival to school, learner will independently put away belongings in designated place in 4/5 opportunities.
- When departing school, learner will independently retrieve belongings from designated place in 4/5 opportunities.
- When departing school, learner will independently don coat and bag in 4/5 opportunities.
- Learner will use credit/debit card or school ID to make purchase, completing 80% of task-analysis steps independently, in 4/5 consecutive opportunities.
- Learner will use multiple types of phone to call familiar numbers (parent, home), dialing 100% of digits independently in 4/5 consecutive opportunities.
- Learner will retrieve and return classroom materials to storage location with 90% accuracy in 4/5 school days.

Toileting

- Learner will void on toilet on schedule in 4/5 consecutive opportunities.
- Learner will indicate need to use toilet and void on toilet in 4/5 consecutive opportunities.
- Learner will clean self after using toilet with decreasing prompts below baseline in 4/5 consecutive opportunities.
- Learner will remain dry between toilet trips for 4/5 days per week for 3 consecutive school weeks.

Hygiene

- Learner will brush teeth, completing 90% of task-analysis steps independently in 4/5 consecutive opportunities.
- Learner will use tissue to blow or wipe nose with/without prompts in 4/5 consecutive opportunities.
- Learner will wash hands before eating, completing 90% of task-analysis steps independently in 4/5 consecutive opportunities.
- Learner will clean up area after eating, completing 90% of task-analysis steps independently in 4/5 consecutive opportunities.

AUTISM GOALS ACROSS THE LIFESPAN FROM ABA SPEECH

GENERAL SAFETY

General Safety

- Learner will stay in designated area in classroom, school building, school yard, community, home settings for increasing durations of time above baseline, in 100% of opportunities, for 4 consecutive school days.
- Learner will ask permission/tell adult before leaving classroom, community/home area in 100% of opportunities, for 9/10 consecutive school days.
- Learner will identify items that may be hot/sharp in picture and in situ with 100% accuracy, for 4 consecutive sessions.
- Learner will avoid items that may be hot/sharp with 100% accuracy, in 4/5 consecutive opportunities.
- Learner will follow classroom procedure when fire/tornado/lock down alarm alerts, completing 100% of steps with or without prompts for 4/5 consecutive opportunities.
- Learner will complete steps of family fire/tornado/other emergency procedure under rehearsal conditions, completing 100% of steps with or without prompts for 4/5 consecutive opportunities.
- Learner will receptively or expressively identify 12 different community helpers based on photo or in situ, with 90% accuracy in 4/5 opportunities.
- Learner will produce identifying information (vocally or via picture/card exchange) when asked by familiar adult, with 100% accuracy in 4/5 opportunities.
- Learner will produce identifying information (vocally or via picture/card exchange) when asked by uniformed or otherwise identifiable community helpers with 100% accuracy, in 4/5 opportunities.

AUTISM GOALS ACROSS THE LIFESPAN FROM ABA SPEECH

ADVOCACY

Advocacy

- Learner will request break, reduced demand or some environmental adjustment when presented with known non-preferred task with or without prompts in 4/5 opportunities for 9/10 consecutive school days.
- Learner will request break, reduced demand or some environmental adjustment when presented with known non-preferred conditions with or without prompts in 4/5 opportunities for 9/10 consecutive school days.
- Learner will ask for clarification from staff regarding classroom instructions or assignments, with or without prompts in 4/5 opportunities for 9/10 consecutive school days.
- Learner will approach familiar or preferred adults and request social attention vocally or using AAC without engaging in disruptive behavior (target #) times/day for 9/10 consecutive school days.
- Learner will approach familiar or preferred adults and request tangible item or activity vocally or using AAC without engaging in disruptive behavior (target #) times/day for 9/10 consecutive school days.
- Learner will identify emotions of others depicted in photo stimuli or in situ, vocally or using AAC, with 90% accuracy in 4/5 consecutive opportunities.
- Learner will identify own emotions including worry/concern, disappointment, satisfaction, excitement/pleasure in relationship to known preferred/non-preferred events using an "I feel ___" statement with 90% correlation in 4/5 consecutive opportunities.

AUTISM GOALS ACROSS THE LIFESPAN FROM ABA SPEECH

EXECUTIVE FUNCTIONING

Coping Behavior

- Given a visual or video model, learner will demonstrate 5 different coping responses under rehearsal/practice conditions in 4/5 consecutive opportunities.
- Given a vocal instruction or request, learner will demonstrate 5 different coping responses under rehearsal/practice conditions in 4/5 consecutive opportunities.
- Learner will demonstrate a preferred coping response under contrived "trigger" conditions, with pre-session planning in 2/3 opportunities for 4 consecutive sessions.
- Learner will demonstrate a preferred coping response under contrived "trigger" conditions without pre-session planning in 2/3 opportunities for 4 consecutive sessions.
- Learner will demonstrate a preferred coping response in the presence of known "trigger," with or without prompts in 4/5 consecutive opportunities.
- Learner will demonstrate a preferred coping response in the presence of known "trigger," with or without prompts without engaging in disruptive behavior in 4/5 consecutive opportunities.

Tolerance

- Learner will complete known non-preferred tasks with or without prompts for increasing durations of time/number of responses above baseline without engaging in disruptive behavior in 90% of opportunities for 3 consecutive weeks.
- Learner will tolerate known short-term unpleasantries with or without prompts for increasing durations of time above baseline without engaging in disruptive behavior in 90% of opportunities for 3 consecutive weeks.
- Learner will tolerate delays or changes to schedule without engaging in disruptive behavior in 90% of opportunities for 3 consecutive weeks.
- Learner will tolerate corrective feedback on classwork or assignment by remaining calm and making requested adjustment, with or without prompts in 90% of opportunities for 3 consecutive weeks.

AUTISM GOALS ACROSS THE LIFESPAN FROM ABA SPEECH

EXECUTIVE FUNCTIONING CONT.

Organization

- Using a developmentally appropriate organizational system, learner will place papers/items into designated binder section/folder with 90% accuracy during massed practice for 4/5 consecutive sessions.
- Using a developmentally appropriate organizational system, learner will place papers/items into designated binder section/folder in situ/classroom setting, with 90% accuracy for observed opportunities in one month.
- Learner will retrieve requested item from binder/folder system when asked in setting within 1 minute of being asked, with 90% accuracy during massed practice for 4/5 consecutive sessions.
- Learner will retrieve requested item from binder/folder system when asked in situ/classroom setting, within 1 minute of being asked, with 90% accuracy for observed opportunities in one month.

Self Monitoring

- Learner will make a tally mark on a teacher-prepared self-monitoring form each time he or she engages in a targeted behavior with 80% accuracy or agreement with staff count for 9/10 consecutive opportunities.
- Learner will report to teacher/staff that they have met predetermined criteria for reinforcement based on self-behavior tally in 9/10 consecutive opportunities.
- Following a disciplinary event, learner will engage in guided conversation with trusted adult, identifying what preceded the event, what their response was, and what the consequence to that response was with decreasing prompts below baseline for 9/10 consecutive opportunities.
- Following a disciplinary event, learner will engage in guided conversation with trusted adult, identifying what preceded the event, provide one alternative response to that event, and what the consequence to that alternative response may be with decreasing prompts below baseline for 9/10 consecutive opportunities.

AUTISM GOALS ACROSS THE LIFESPAN FROM ABA SPEECH

EXECUTIVE FUNCTIONING CONT.

Planning

- Learner will record assignments in self-selected planning tool with or without a visual model for 90% of assignments for 3 consecutive school weeks.
- Learner will pack backpack at end of school day with all needed materials based on assigned homework tasks listed in planner with or without visual checklist in 90% of opportunities for 3 consecutive school weeks.
- Learner will complete novel short-term academic task (can be completed in 1 class period) from list of steps created by teacher without prompts in 9/10 consecutive opportunities.
- Learner will complete novel long-term academic task (completed over span of several work periods) from list of steps created by teacher without prompts in 9/10 consecutive opportunities.
- Learner will break down short familiar task (completed in 15 min/less) into checklist of steps with decreasing prompts below baseline in 4/5 consecutive opportunities.
- Learner will break down long-term familiar task (completed over span of several work periods) into checklist of steps with decreasing prompts below baseline in 4/5 consecutive opportunities.
- Learner will complete novel long-term academic task (completed over span of several work periods) from self-created list of steps with decreasing prompts below baseline in 4/5 consecutive opportunities.

About the Author

Rose Griffin, MA, CCC-SLP, BCBA, is a certified speech-language pathologist (SLP) and board certified behavior analyst (BCBA) with a passion for helping SLPs, BCBAs, and RBTs work together to support all autistic learners. She is the founder of ABA Speech, an organization dedicated to professional development that unites teams—and transforms communication through customized consultations, engaging training and the ABA Speech Connection CEU Membership. Rose is also the host of the popular ABA Speech Podcast, where she shares practical strategies. A highly sought-after speaker, she enjoys connecting with professionals at the local, state, and national levels. At the heart of Rose's work is the mission of ABA Speech: building better learner outcomes by better collaboration.

Index

Note: Pages in *italics* refer to figures.

Wiley The manufacturer's authorized representative according to the EU
General Product Safety Regulation is Wiley-VCH GmbH, Boschstr. 12,
69469 Weinheim, Germany, e-mail: Product_Safety@wiley.com.

Printed and bound by CPI Group (UK) Ltd, Croydon, CR0 4YY

14/06/2026

02138091-0001